DANIEL PLOOF

LAMENT

100 PRAYERS of SELF-REFLECTION, CONFESSION, and MEDITATION

Psalm51 PUBLISHING

GALLATIN, TENNESSEE

Lament: 100 Prayers of Self-Reflection, Confession, and
Meditation
Copyright © 2026 by Daniel Ploof

All Rights Reserved. No part of this publication may be
reproduced, distributed, or transmitted in any form or by
any means, including photocopying, recording, or other
electronic or mechanical methods, without the prior written
permission of the publisher, except as permitted by U.S.
copyright law.

Library of Congress Control Number: 2026908908

ISBN: 978-1-966758-05-1 (print)

Scripture quotations are from the ESV® Bible (The Holy
Bible, English Standard Version®), © 2001 by Crossway, a
publishing ministry of Good News Publishers. Used by
permission. All rights reserved.

Cover Design: @creativeiro
Cover Image: Elisabeth Jurenka

CONTENTS

Lost in the Wilderness

I have always been drawn to self-reflective prayers in the Bible. I find it incredibly comforting when I read about ordinary people like me who bear their souls before the Lord. There is no shame in their cries for help because their sanity hangs in the balance. They are physically, mentally, and emotionally exhausted, evident from the desperation of their hearts. I can certainly relate to their depravity. I have found myself in similar valleys of despair throughout my life and wondered if rescue and reprieve would ever come my way. For the desert of life can be a barren wasteland at times, and I am ill-equipped to survive all alone in it. That is why I must learn to express my emotions instead of allowing them to keep me chained to hopelessness.

Satan has a way of tempting me to believe that I am the only one struggling with a particular trial. Isolation has always been his strategy of attack because he knows how vulnerable I am when separated from accountability. I can lose all sense of direction if I am not careful and fall victim to wandering off-course without proper guidance. Thus, I need God's Word to not only chart my course unto righteousness but lead me towards my true north: Jesus Christ. Far too often, I believe I am prepared to venture into the wilderness, but my priorities often get mixed up before beginning the journey. I cannot seem to remember that I need a map and compass to know where I'm headed. As a result, I often make wrong turns and enter dangerous terrain unknowingly.

What is most concerning about getting lost in the wilderness is that I assume I am okay when clearly I'm not. Self-deception takes over and I lean more on my own understanding instead of relying upon the Holy Spirit to guide my path. It is natural to think only of myself and yield to pride. My naïve attitude puts me in positions where my only hope is to cry out to the Lord for rescue. It is a humbling experience thinking I know better only to fall flat on my face and own my foolishness. The path towards righteousness is straight and narrow, but I am more apt to choose the winding road of temptation rather than trust the Spirit. Why do I make things harder on myself than I should? Why can I not stick to God's plan for my life and surrender to His sovereignty?

It is fairly easy to get lost in the wilderness of my mind. The enemy knows which buttons to push to fluster my thoughts and play with my emotions. He tempts me to panic in the deepest parts of my soul and question whether life is worth living. I have mourned the consequences of my sins and sought reconciliation with others, but I still feel lost at times. Sanctification often feels more like 1-step forward and 2-steps back. I long to be free from Satan's scarlet letter but past sins continue to plague my future. The moment I think I have turned a page, I default into old patterns and lose valuable momentum.

Those are the moments when I offer my blunt and honest thoughts to the Lord and own the depths of my depravity. In His grace, He allows me to lament the difficulty of my trials and bear my soul through raw and unfiltered prayers. The Lord is not put off by the intensity of my emotions. Rather, He speaks peace to my weary soul and cleanses my mind with absolute truth. He calms my heart by reminding me that I am His child—unconditionally loved and accepted despite my past failures. It is why I love self-reflective prayers because they are a window into my mind and an opportunity to preach the Gospel to myself.

They allow me ample opportunity to release pent up feelings and questions I have long been harboring. I can cast fear, doubt, and worry at the foot of the cross by mourning the trials I am facing. No matter what the future holds, blunt and honest prayers remind me that God almighty sits on the throne of eternity. He will never allow harm to come upon me because my future is sealed by the blood of His Son. Granted, trials will surely come and go, but His steadfast love endures forever and will sustain me through the trials of life.

INTRODUCTION
Lament Inspired

What is a self-reflective prayer? It is an opportunity to purge our thoughts and feelings at the foot of the cross and preach the Gospel to ourselves to calm our minds and soothe our troubled hearts. Self-reflective prayers are meant to confront the enormity of trials and counter spiritual warfare with the absolute truth of Holy Scripture. Not a day goes by where we are not immersed in a spiritual battle, for war which rages in the spiritual realm carries far greater implications than we realize. As such, we must not only acknowledge that war exists but prepare for battle by learning how to cleanse our minds with Jesus' Gospel of salvation.

Satan is a mastermind who tempts us to wallow in guilt, shame, and regret. He knows that if we dwell upon our unworthiness, we will yield to sin and give up on God. For if we believe all hope is lost, what need is there to repent? That is the crux of the enemy's tactic, and we are wise to guard our hearts from believing such lies. We are never too far gone for the grace of God to cleanse us from all unrighteousness. It may not feel like it in the moment, but His mercies are new every morning and we must wait in expectant hope for the sun to rise once again. When it does, the clouds of darkness will dissipate and burn away from our conscience like morning fog in the sunrise. No longer will we be bound by sin but set free to worship the Lord.

Lament-inspired prayers are deeply personal. All we need is to be humble, vulnerable, and teachable by God's grace. Keep in mind, we are not meant to camp out in the valley but to resist acting as if everything is fine when clearly it is not. Such prayers face reality head-on with wisdom from God's Word to cleanse our minds. They answer misperceptions with absolute truth and help make sense of our trials.

Truly, we will never experience reprieve from Satan's schemes if we are dishonest with ourselves. However, we will never discover freedom if we do not bow our knees at the foot of the cross either.

This anthology of 100 prayers is meant to help us begin the process of self-reflection, confession, and meditation. They are not exhaustive prayers but personal examples to point us in the right direction as we express our hearts to God and face reality. The worst thing we could do in our journey of faith is bottle-up our emotions. The enemy thrives in environments where absolute truth is nowhere to be found. If we never address our thoughts and feelings, there is no need to remedy them. Therefore, we must meet the Lord in the valley of despair and allow Him to minister to our broken hearts.

God does not call us from the mountain's peak to meet Him there when we get our act together. Rather, He walks with us in the valley so we will not be consumed. The Father's love for us knows no bounds. It is supernatural and holds the power to cleanse us from sin and lead us home to everlasting life. Whether we realize it or not, the prayers we often utter are similar to prayers of lament. However, we tend to leave out one factor when we purge our hearts of raw emotion: absolute truth. Without it, we are merely venting our spleen and are subject to unrealistic expectations which lead nowhere but keep us continually frustrated, bitter, and discontent.

Self-preaching must be the backbone of our prayers, for it centers our minds on the truth of the Gospel and guards us against temptation. Without the sword of the Spirit, we have no other way to defeat the enemy. Therefore, we must abide in Christ each day as the Spirit wages war against the forces of darkness on our behalf. Jesus said, **"I am the way, and the truth, and the life. No one comes to the Father except through me (John 14:6)**. As such, let us not forget that He is the answer to our problems and will make all things new for those who trust in Him alone for salvation. However, we must come to Him in humble reverence to find healing for our weary and troubled souls.

Lost and Found

(Confusion)

"For evils have encompassed me beyond number; my iniquities have
overtaken me, and I cannot see; they are more than the hairs
of my head; my heart fails me."

— *Psalm 40:12* —

Lord, I am hopelessly lost in the wilderness of my mind. No matter where life takes me, everything looks the same. All I see are trees, bushes, and an endless canopy of grey clouds to block the sun. My days are wrought with fear. How will I survive? Will I ever be rescued? With each passing day, I am reminded of how foolish I have been. The wake of destruction I've caused still haunts me. Foolishly, I lost sight of the trailhead long ago and am now paying the price for wandering far off-course. I cannot distinguish right from wrong anymore. My conscience feels seared. It is as if my moral compass is broken and I lost sight of where true north lies. I never realized how ill-equipped I was to survive the rugged wilderness alone, but sin has left me vulnerable to attack and predators lurk in the shadows waiting to devour my flesh.

Despite my failures and iniquities, Your Spirit reminds me that I am Yours. I am never alone because You walk beside me through the fire. Thank You for convicting my heart by the power of Your Word. Sin's stronghold holds no power over me because You bring light into the darkness of my heart. I praise You for leading me along paths of righteousness to refresh my weary soul. I am cleansed by the healing waters of grace and mercy which You lavishly provide. Thank You for meeting my needs, Lord. No matter how lost I feel, I am found in Your loving arms because You died to set me free. Thus, I shall not fear the terror of the night but rest peacefully in the light of Your saving grace and mercy forevermore. Amen.

Without Hesitation

(Hesitancy)

"And Jesus, looking at him, loved him, and said to him, 'You lack one thing: go, sell all that you have and give to the poor, and you will have treasure in heaven; and come, follow me.' Disheartened by the saying, he went away sorrowful, for he had great possessions."

— Mark 10:21–22 —

Lord, the path of salvation seems easy to walk at times, but I do not know whether I can take up my cross and follow You. What You call me to sacrifice has always given me a false sense of security. Why must I let it go? It does not feel like my possessions are a hindrance or burden to following You, but that is obviously not the case. If I am honest, what frightens me is completely letting go of everything I hold dear to trust Your Word. My heart knows Your promises are true, but my mind continues to default into self-protection mode, reminding me that I need an alternative plan to fall back on. Why is it so hard to let go? I do not want false idols in my life, but there appears to be a barrier between us which is causing me to pause and hesitate rather than trust Your Word wholeheartedly.

Nevertheless, You welcome me into Your presence. I am honored to be called Your precious child. Help me relinquish control of my life and trust Your sovereign will. The enemy would have me believe I am divided within, but that is a lie. You saved my soul for eternity. I am no longer held captive by sin but set free to serve and worship You. No matter where I go, I am certain that what You ask me to sacrifice will never compare to the blessings which await in heaven one day. I am secure in my salvation and that is all the assurance I need to follow You when You call my name. Help me take up my cross and trust Your Spirit wherever You lead, no matter the cost. Amen.

Faith over Fear

(Fear)

"When I am afraid, I put my trust in you. In God, whose word I praise,
in God I trust; I shall not be afraid. What can flesh do to me?"

— *Psalm 56:3–4* —

Lord, why am I so afraid? I may put up a good front to others, but You know how much I wrestle with fear inside. In many ways, the future scares me. I cannot control what lies ahead but only accept what comes my way. Like a hamster on a wheel, I am consumed with worry to the point where my spirit is broken. I have lost all hope that tomorrow will be any different. My mind filters everything through a glass-half-empty lens where I expect bad things to happen at any given moment. Why am I so frightened? Why do I lack mustard seed faith to trust where You lead me? Satan holds no power unless I give him opportunity, yet I continue to let down my guard and welcome him in. How could I be so foolish? All he speaks are lies meant to keep me isolated so I default to unhealthy coping mechanisms. I do not want to feel alone anymore, but I am terrified of what the future may bring if I do not try to control it.

Regardless of my fear and worry, You calm my mind with a yoke of contentment. In exchange for my bondage, You bring peace to my restless soul. I am made courageous by the power of Your shed blood which crushed the serpent's head. No longer am I bound by fear but set free to proclaim the joy of my salvation. You prepare a table before me in the presence of my enemies. My hope is in You and I shall not be afraid of future trials because You are ever-present. I trust Your sovereignty and will align my heart to Yours so that I walk by faith and not by sight. You are the wellspring of my soul and I will trust You no matter what tomorrow might bring. Amen.

Insecure, yet Confident

(Insecurity)

"For we do not have a high priest who is unable to sympathize with our weaknesses, but one who in every respect has been tempted as we are, yet without sin. Let us then with confidence draw near to the throne of grace, that we may receive mercy and find grace to help in time of need."

— Hebrews 4:15–16 —

Lord, the pleasures of this world are comfortable and familiar for a reason. The enemy knows that if I expect them to fulfill me, I will have no reason to trust You. The best this world has to offer cannot compare to Your provision. I know that but am still drawn to worldly pleasures like a moth to a flame. Insecurity has become an idol in my heart and I am held captive by its deadly snare. I am worried that my strength will fail when I must stand firm. I need self-control to say, "No!" when temptation comes, but I have been conditioned to sin for so long that my coping mechanism kicks in when stress and anxiety overwhelm me. It is as if I have no clue how to respond to worry in a healthy manner. I just default to the path of least resistance and yield to fleshly cravings to dull the pain.

However, You give me confidence to stand boldly amid adversity and not be shaken. Despite my weakness, I am born-again by the blood of Jesus and empowered to destroy strongholds which seek to enslave my flesh. All that I need was provided when You came to earth and died in my place. You have given me assurance that I do not need false idols to make me happy. I must not succumb to insecurity to appease my uncertainty either. Rather, I can be fully confident knowing You stood in my place and endured all of the temptations this world has to offer without yielding to sin. Thank You for proving that I do not need false idols in my life to feel safe and secure. Amen.

Waves of Doubt

(Doubt)

"If any of you lacks wisdom, let him ask God, who gives generously to all without reproach, and it will be given him. But let him ask in faith, with no doubting, for the one who doubts is like a wave of the sea that is driven and tossed by the wind."

— James 1:5–6 —

Lord, it seems as if trials magnify my unbelief more than anything else. I never could have imagined that a lack of faith would be my greatest downfall, but doubt is the reason my life is in disarray. I tend to waver when it comes to staking my life on the inerrancy of Your Word. Some things are hard to accept, such as enduring persecution for Your Gospel or taking a bold stand on issues of morality. I also struggle yielding to feelings which cloud my judgment regarding what is truly sinful. I do not want to doubt Scripture, but it feels like culture is pressing me to compromise my faith. How should I respond? Am I allowed to doubt Scripture without undermining my faith altogether, or is faith a package deal of completely trusting You and Your Word?

I am reminded that I must not lean on my own understanding but trust You with all my heart (Prov. 3:5), for it will be healing to my flesh and refreshment to my bones (Prov. 3:8). I am humbled by the grace You lavishly pour out on my weary heart. The amount of spiritual warfare swirling around is enough to make me throw in the towel altogether on my faith. Nevertheless, my soul is not dissuaded by the schemes of the enemy. Rather, it is emboldened for the Gospel and steadfast in its belief that Scripture is 100% absolute truth. Thus, when I take a stand on issues of right and wrong, it is not I who judges or speaks conviction but the Lord who spoke creation into existence and is the final authority on issues of morality. Amen.

Guilt Offering
(Guilt)

"For all have sinned and fall short of the glory of God, and are justified by his grace as a gift, through the redemption that is in Christ Jesus."

— Romans 3:23–24 —

Lord, my soul is weary from guilt I harbor deep inside. I have fallen woefully short of the righteous standard You expect from me. Sin weighs heavy on my conscience and I am painfully aware of how far I have fallen from grace. As King David declared, **"Against you, you only, have I sinned and done what is evil in your sight, so that you may be justified in your words and blameless in your judgment" (Psalm 51:4)**. Guilt has become a scarlet letter I cannot avoid. I know full well the wrongs I have done. I have tasted the filth of temptation when I chose to rebel against Your Word. There are no excuses to justify my actions. I own the poor decisions I made and the consequences of my foolishness. The memories of sin are a constant companion, though I wish I could go back in time and reject temptation rather than yield to my desires.

Despite my wicked heart, You cleanse my soul with forgiveness. When I repent of my sins, You completely pardon my offenses. Truly, I am unworthy of second chances, yet You extend an olive branch to me when I least deserve it. How can I accept such a priceless gift? My life is nothing more than a collection of empty promises to go and sin no more (John 8:11), but all I do is fall short of honoring my commitment. There is nothing which concerns You more than the condition of my broken and contrite heart. Therefore, help me come to You in reverence to receive pardon for my guilt offering. Your grace is more than enough to make me whole again, and I pray that I never take Your forgiveness from granted again. Amen.

Depths of Despair

(Despair)

"We are afflicted in every way but not crushed; perplexed but not driven to despair; persecuted but not forsaken; struck down but not destroyed."

— 2 Corinthians 4:8–9 —

Lord, it goes without saying that I am afflicted in every way. The scars I bear testify to poor choices I have made throughout my life. When I look around, I see nothing but pain and sorrow. I fear the depths of depression that have overtaken my soul. Hopelessness is my constant companion, dysfunctional as it may be. Emotions are also the driving force in my life, guiding my path toward giving up on life itself. Satan is quick to tempt me with suicidal thoughts to ease the immense weight I carry. Visions of sinful regrets haunt my dreams. It seems that rescue and reprieve are sources of nourishment I will never discover among this desert wilderness. I am parched with weariness and do not know whether I can make it another day, let alone a lifetime.

Even still, Your Word reminds me that I am helpless to defeat the enemy alone, for only by the power of Your Spirit am I empowered to reject his wicked schemes and stand victorious on judgment day. Satan knows how to overwhelm my mind with fear, doubt, and worry, but You draw me into the light and break the chains which bind my heart. Isolation has plunged my mind into depths of darkness I never dreamt were possible. The thought of taking matters into my own hands and ending my life has crossed my mind more than I care to admit. As such, I have learned that my true identity is not found in the scarlet letter of pain and sorrow but the saving grace and mercy of Jesus Christ. Indeed, despair may last for a long and dark season, but I will not be tempted to believe it will last a lifetime. You hold my life in the palm of Your hands and I will trust You forevermore. Amen.

Tired and Weary

(Fatigue)

*"Come to me, all who labor and are heavy laden, and I will give you rest.
Take my yoke upon you, and learn from me, for I am gentle
and lowly in heart, and you will find rest for your souls.
For my yoke is easy, and my burden is light."*

— *Matthew 11:28–30* —

Lord, I am tired. It is amazing how one simple word can summarize the way I feel every day of my life. It is difficult to put into words what it means for me to be so weary. My body aches for rest while my mind needs to shut off and decompress from all of life's pressures I am struggling to manage. There is not enough time in the day to check off everything on my to-do list, and that bothers me. No one expects me to be perfect, but I place tremendous expectations upon myself to bear the load of responsibility for my success or failure. What I have come to realize is that I am dangerously close to my breaking point. Stress runs high and my nerves are shot, more often than not. It seems I do not know how to get off the hamster's wheel and stop worrying about what I cannot control.

My fatigue comes as no surprise to You, of course. You patiently wait for me to stop carrying the full weight of responsibility and trust You instead to shoulder my burdens. I do not understand why it is so difficult for me to let go, but I pray that You intercede on my behalf before it is too late. I cannot fathom what it looks or feels like to trade my yoke of fatigue for the rest You promise, but I heartily accept Your gift of peace which my soul needs. For too long, pride has been the culprit of why I have not entrusted in You to carry my burdens. As such, teach me to release my grip from stress and anxiety so I may not be crushed by fatigue but find rest for my aching soul. Amen.

House of Mourning
(Repentance)

"It is better to go to the house of mourning than to go to the house of feasting, for this is the end of all mankind, and the living will lay it to heart."

— *Ecclesiastes 7:2* —

Lord, why do I act as if everything is fine when clearly it is not? I often think more highly of myself than I ought. Sin has become comfortable in my life and I fear that I have lost touch with reality. I do not come remotely close to mourning or loathing my sins. Rather, I minimize, justify, or discredit any notion that they are a concern. I treat them as a viral infection rather than cancer, and the residual effect is that I need open heart surgery to save my life. Nowhere is this more evident than in my day-to-day actions where I feel little to no remorse for how my behavior affects others. I act as if my sins exist in a bubble, cut off from direct contact with those around me. Unfortunately, I do more damage than good when I act as if I am a devout Christ-follower yet live in direct opposition to Your moral law.

What I need is to mourn my sin and lament over damages I have caused. Apologies are meaningless if I fail to recognize the depth and breadth of my foolishness. You died to set me free from the grips of hell, yet I take Your grace for granted every time I choose to disobey Your will for my life. You take no pleasure judging me for my sins, but I thank You for helping me recognize the far-reaching impact of my transgressions. I cannot call myself a Christian yet live to please myself, Help me mourn my poor choices and take responsibility for the consequences of my actions. You made a way to set me free from sin and death, and I praise You for providing ample opportunity to humble myself, repent of my sins, and live for righteousness. Amen.

Slow to Anger

(Anger)

"A hot-tempered man stirs up strife,
but he who is slow to anger quiets contention."

— Proverbs 15:18 —

Lord, anger is an emotion I know all too well. When life does not turn out the way I think it should, I allow my emotions to get the best of me and lash out against others. Rather than relinquish control of my unrighteous anger to You, I harbor it deep within my heart and continue to feed its unquenchable fire. What's even worse is I funnel other emotions through anger so that all my loved ones experience is wrath and fury instead of love and grace. My lack of self-control in this area is arguably my greatest regret. Things I have said and done by lashing out in frustration or bitterness only prove the immaturity of my faith. I do not want others to walk on eggshells around me, but I can see the fear in their eyes as they brace for the inevitable outburst. Oh, how I wish I could turn back time and guard my tongue, but all I feel are guilt and shame for wounds I have inflicted upon others.

Regret is a powerful emotion. It can illicit heart change or plunge one deeper into the valley of despair. While I certainly regret the times I allowed anger to overcome my mind, I know You will not abandon me. Your wrath is kindled every time I sin, but You choose to punish Your Son rather than cast me into the darkness for eternity. I will never fully comprehend how much You love me to make such a sacrifice. It is enough to shatter my pride and break my wayward heart. I am inspired to change my wicked ways because unrighteous anger is not befitting of a Christ-follower. Instead, You call me to love others unconditionally and maintain self-control over my emotions so I do not relent to anger and frustration again. Amen.

Never Alone

(Loneliness)

*"Fear not, for I am with you; be not dismayed, for I am your God;
I will strengthen you, I will help you, I will uphold you
with my righteous right hand."*

— *Isaiah 41:10* —

Lord, though I am surrounded by people on a daily basis, I feel so alone. Solitude can be beneficial at times, but isolation has allowed the enemy to overwhelm my mind with doubt. I doubt whether I am loved and respected. I doubt if I have value in this world. I doubt if You have a plan and purpose for my life, and I doubt whether the loneliness I feel will ever go away. Truly, I can get hopelessly lost in the wilderness of my mind. The more I dwell upon how isolated I feel, the closer I get to giving up on life altogether. The silence I feel is deafening and I cannot escape the terrors of the night which haunt my dreams. Satan has a stranglehold on my psyche. The more I try to escape, the tighter his chains become as they dig into my skin and constrict my ability to breathe or even think clearly.

But You, O Lord, are the anchor of my soul. You ground me in truth to dispel the enemy's lies. I can feel the cool whisper of Your Spirit quenching the flames of loneliness around my heart. Though I may be isolated, I am not alone for You are with me. Your shield of faith (Eph. 6:16) guards my weary soul from doubt and reminds me of Your unending promise to never leave or forsake me in my hour of need. I am completely dependent upon Your grace and mercy to live another day. They are the lifeblood of my salvation and I thank You for loving me enough to release the chains which bind my heart. You give me strength when my hope fails, for joy comes in the morning to those who trust in the name of the Lord for salvation. Amen.

Not Ashamed

(Shame)

"For whoever is ashamed of me and of my words in this adulterous and sinful generation, of him will the Son of Man also be ashamed when he comes in the glory of his Father with the holy angels."

— Mark 8:38 —

Lord, it seems foolish to identify myself as a Christian yet live ashamed of the Gospel. Why would I call upon Your name for salvation but reject Your Word which tells me everything I need to know about who You are, why You came, and what You preached? I would be naïve to assume Scripture is powerless against the enemy, yet I struggle remembering that fact. I have no issue accepting You as my Savior but making You Lord of my life is much harder. It requires me to surrender my pride and yield to Your sovereign authority which is easier said than done to my selfish heart. I struggle abiding in You (John 15:4-7) and defending Your Word in spite of opposition. I am afraid of being persecuted for my faith, and that has caused me to water down the Gospel and dismiss Your Word as absolute truth.

This culture is indeed sinful and adulterous. Satan has successfully baited me into being more concerned about cultural acceptance than serving You. As a result, I have missed golden opportunities to plant seeds of righteousness throughout my life. Help me break that trend. I do not want to be a Christian by name alone. Rather, I want my good works to glorify You. I am tired of being lukewarm in my faith. I need spiritual revival to ignite in my soul so others may come to know You better. I am nothing without You, Lord, so help me live out my faith with boldness. **"For I am not ashamed of the gospel, for it is the power of God for salvation to everyone who believes" (Romans 1:16).** Amen.

Weight of the World

(Anxiety)

*"Anxiety in a man's heart weighs him down,
but a good word makes him glad."*

— *Proverbs 12:25* —

Lord, I feel like I am carrying an eight-hundred-pound gorilla on my back. Whether it be physical, emotional, or psychological, the weight I am holding is unbearable. It has the potential of landing me in the hospital if I am not careful. My nerves are shot. I have difficulty sleeping at night. My appetite is extreme and my attitude is erratic to say the least. One more straw will surely break the camel's back if I do not seek intervention quickly. Truly, I do not understand why I bear the burdens of others. Rarely is the same sentiment reciprocated in my direction, but I am expected to hold everyone else's baggage and bear the brunt of stress and anxiety. I am tired of sacrificing my time, energy, and resources. I have far too much on my own plate and no one to offload responsibility so I can find rest.

My self-focused attitude is a recipe for disaster, though. It is easy for me to look in the mirror and act as if I am everyone else's personal savior. I could not fathom measuring up to that standard. That is why I need You, Lord, to ease this weight of anxiety which is crushing me. I do not want to complain about life but appreciate the opportunities You provide to minister to others. Help me wash my mind with the promises of Your Word which remind me that this world is not my home. The afflictions I bear are momentary in the grand scheme of creation. Therefore, I will count my trials as joy because You are sanctifying me through them. Your Word is all the encouragement I need to survive today and live for tomorrow, so help me clear my mind of anxiety and focus on Jesus instead. Amen.

Bitter Jealousy

(Jealousy)

"But if you have bitter jealousy and selfish ambition in your hearts, do not boast and be false to the truth. This is not the wisdom that comes down from above, but is earthly, unspiritual, demonic. For where jealousy and selfish ambition exist, there will be disorder and every vile practice."

— *James 3:14–16* —

Lord, I would not consider myself a jealous person, but lately I have been consumed with comparing myself to others. I am far too concerned with what I look like, the things I own, and the friends and family I keep. I see the success and victories of others and covet the joy they must be experiencing. It only magnifies my shortcomings and failures and makes me jealous of what I lack to be happy. I know there is no pleasure in this world which can satisfy my soul. Nothing can compare to the joy of my salvation, yet I continually find my mind drifting to worldly pleasures and coveting my neighbor. Selfish ambition is destroying me from within, and I must change my ways or suffer the grave consequences of my actions.

Why am I so discontent? Your provision is perfect, but I struggle recognizing it when trials overwhelm my psyche. I have lost sight of what is most important: repenting of my sins and giving my life to You. Self-centeredness is all I am focused on, though. Please forgive me for putting fleshly desires above You. Jealousy has become an idol in my heart and caused me to complain about my lot in the life rather than thanking You for Your provision. My life is best served when I put the joy of my salvation in proper perspective. As such, give me eyes to see beauty in the ashes of my life, for You work all things together for my good. I commit to counting my blessings daily, not out of duty or obligation but from a thankful heart indebted to Christ. Amen.

No Regrets

(Regret)

"Brothers, I do not consider that I have made it my own.
But one thing I do: forgetting what lies behind and straining forward
to what lies ahead, I press on toward the goal for the prize
of the upward call of God in Christ Jesus."

— Philippians 3:13–14 —

Lord, there are a lot of poor decisions I regret. I wish I could go back in time and change my ways, but I can't. For better or worse, who I am yesterday and today are forever intertwined. Past failures have shaped my character, and I stand before You broken over sin but healed by Your amazing grace. In spite of this, the enemy baits me into questioning whether I am truly forgiven. Have I learned from the sins of my past? It is easy to doubt the genuineness of my repentance when I continue to sin against You. **"For I do not understand my own actions. For I do not do what I want, but I do the very thing I hate" (Romans 7:15)**. I cannot seem to avoid yielding to temptation throughout my life. How then can I break free from sin to avoid being defeated by guilt, shame, and regret?

While I lament many things in life, I do not regret my decision to trust Your Word. You remind me that **"for those who love God all things work together for good, for those who are called according to his purpose" (Romans 8:28)**. What Satan intended for evil, You used to restore and redeem my lost soul. Sin magnified my desperate need for You, and I am healed today because You broke the chains which bound my foolish heart. There are no words to express the depth of gratitude I have for Your salvation. I am certainly being sanctified by Your grace, but I know Your love is real because You forgive my sins each time I repent of my transgressions. Amen.

Constant Reminder

(Irritation)

"So to keep me from becoming conceited because of the surpassing greatness of the revelations, a thorn was given me in the flesh, a messenger of Satan to harass me, to keep me from becoming conceited. Three times I pleaded with the Lord about this, that it should leave me. But he said to me, 'My grace is sufficient for you, for my power is made perfect in weakness.'"

— 2 Corinthians 12:7–9 —

Lord, spiritual warfare is intense for me these days. No matter how hard I cling to the promises of Your Word, I cannot escape the flaming arrows of the enemy. Satan is relentless in his pursuit of my soul and this thorn in the flesh is greatly irritating me. I find no reprieve from it—only pain and torment. It is difficult to count my trials as joy because there appears to be no end in sight to suffering. I feel mocked by the enemy and, to top it all off, You refuse to release me from these chains. Why? I realize that when I am weak I am made strong, but I cannot wrap my mind around the divine purpose of why You would allow affliction to persist in my life.

Weaknesses keep me solely dependent upon Your saving grace for survival in this world. Thank You for teaching me that life's difficulties are an opportunity to grow closer to You. I tend to complain about hardships far too often rather than looking for the silver lining of blessings hidden beneath the surface. Knowing gold is purified by fire comforts me. It helps me rest peacefully in the eye of the storm instead of running away from it. As such, help me trust the plan and purpose You have for my life which includes persecution, pain, and suffering. You have never failed me, Lord, and You never will. To Christ be the glory for enduring the cross on my behalf, for I have been set free by the immeasurable power of Your saving love. Amen.

Silence in Waiting

(Patience)

*"I wait for the LORD, my soul waits, and in his word I hope;
my soul waits for the Lord more than watchmen for the morning,
more than watchmen for the morning."*

— *Psalm 130:5–6* —

Lord, when I am lost in the wilderness of my mind, silence can be deafening. I am overwhelmed by questions which seem to have no definitive answers. Patience does not come naturally to me. Anxiety tends to well up inside when I reflect upon trials before me. What must I do? Who will I trust? Why am I made to suffer? How will all of this work together for my good? It is difficult to trust that an oasis awaits on the other side of the horizon, ready to replenish my mind, body, and soul if I can get there. I cannot see it no matter how hard I try. I assume it is all a part of Your master plan to get me to walk by faith and not by sight. I still have doubts, though. When I pray, it seems You cannot hear me because I receive no response. Why then should I continue to call upon Your name for salvation in my darkest hours?

Psalm 130:5-6 reminds me that I cannot control the future, but I can trust Your sovereign will for my life. The only guaranty I have in life is the truth of Your Word which reminds me I am never alone or forsaken. Thank You for hearing me when I cry for help. I may not always express my gratitude, but I appreciate Your faithfulness as I walk difficult roads and endure suffering. I am not one to wait patiently for answers, but I know You will lead me in ways I cannot fully comprehend in the moment. What I need is hindsight perspective to help me understand why I must wait for You rather than push my agenda. Therefore, help me rest in the discomfort of silence so I can hear Your Spirit whispering hope and healing to my heart. Amen.

Aftermath of Betrayal

(Betrayal)

"A false witness will not go unpunished,
and he who breathes out lies will not escape."

— Proverbs 19:5 —

Lord, wounds cuts deep and I am suffering from the aftermath of betrayal in my life. I do not take trust for granted. I have been burned more than once and know how it feels to place faith in others yet be sorely disappointed based on the consequences of their actions. I do not want to harbor bitterness or resentment in my heart, but I am struggling to keep my emotions in check. Anger has welled up deep within me and I want nothing more than to retaliate for wrongs done against me. I cannot begin to understand why someone I love would betray my trust and sin so grievously. My flesh longs to drink from the cup of retribution, but I know that vengeance is not my cross to bear. Nevertheless, I am fighting to keep my emotions in check and not lash out in unrighteous anger.

Though Satan would have me take matters into my own hands, no good comes when I attempt to become judge, jury, and executioner. With each finger I point, I am convicted at how I betray the trust of others as well. I may be justified in harboring resentment, but it is not Your will for my life. Instead, You call me to love the unlovable and forgive the unforgiveable, because I am no better than those I heap judgment upon. It is far too easy to think more highly of myself than I ought when I have been betrayed, but that is not how I want to be. I want to live free from the shackles of retribution, so help me let go of any desire to take back control from You. Vengeance is Yours and I will not interfere with Your wrath but love my enemies so I do not react in unrighteous anger. Amen.

State of Confusion

(Confusion)

"Beloved, do not believe every spirit, but test the spirits to see whether they are from God, for many false prophets have gone out into the world."

— 1 John 4:1 —

Lord, there are so many voices in my head that I cannot make sense of what is true or not. The enemy has clouded my judgment and baited me into believing that what I hear being preached by culture is gospel truth. The problem is I cannot distinguish fact from fiction. My itching ears are far more inclined to listen to what is self-serving and pleasurable than what I need to hear for spiritual growth and sanctification. I know that the amount of time I spend reading Your Word is a litmus test for moral judgment. I cannot distinguish what is fake if I lack first-hand knowledge of what is true, and that applies to my spiritual walk as well. I must study the original in order to identify a counterfeit, so I am not led astray by false teachings but emboldened in my faith and trust of Holy Scripture as Your moral law.

I confess that I have done a poor job testing whether what I see and hear are from You or the devil. Satan can easily manipulate my mind to think You are speaking to me when clearly You're not. That strategy proved successful in the Garden of Eden and it works to this day when I assume I am filled with knowledge but lack foundational roots from Scripture itself. Spiritual discipline is essential to survival and I need Your help carving out a dedicated time and place to study Your Word and pray for wisdom and understanding. I do not want to be someone who cannot discern right from wrong nor defend their faith amid persecution. In turn, give me clarity in spite of confusion so I may be properly equipped to test the spirits and determine whether they are truly from heaven or the gates of hell. Amen.

Overwhelmed by Guilt
(Guilt)

"You have put me in the depths of the pit, in the regions dark and deep. Your wrath lies heavy upon me, and you overwhelm me with all your waves."

— Psalm 88:6–7 —

Lord, darkness overwhelms my soul. I am crushed by the weight of guilt and shame. The valley of despair is cold and damp, and I have no ability to stay warm. My body shivers from sin's impact in my life—a constant reminder of the consequences of my actions. I have no one to blame but myself for yielding to temptation. No one forced my hand. I chose to sin and must now suffer for damages inflicted upon those I love. Never could I have dreamt I would be so weak of heart and mind. I face fork-in-the-road decisions every day. Why was I so easily misled to sin against You? I know the path of righteousness set before me in Your Word. It is clear and unquestionable, yet I act as if there is some fine-print clause which excludes me from judgment as I live for sinful pleasure. How could I be so naïve?

How frustrated You must be watching me destroy myself time and again! Your patience is incredible. Thank You for continually allowing me to see the error of my ways. Help me modify my behavior so I stop making the same poor decisions. Sometimes, mistakes are made which are unplanned, but sin is different and I know that. When I sin, I am choosing to disobey Scripture. Please forgive my wickedness. Your lovingkindness to me is indescribable. Why You continue to forgive me when I should know better is a mystery. I am so grateful for Your mercy. In turn, help me own my sins, 100%, so I no longer sin against You but honor the sacrifice Your Son made for my salvation. I love You, Lord. Please accept this humble sinner's cry for help. Amen.

Countless Distractions

(Busyness)

"Now as they went on their way, Jesus entered a village. And a woman named Martha welcomed him into her house. And she had a sister called Mary, who sat at the Lord's feet and listened to his teaching. But Martha was distracted with much serving. And she went up to him and said, 'Lord, do you not care that my sister has left me to serve alone? Tell her then to help me.' But the Lord answered her, 'Martha, Martha, you are anxious and troubled about many things, but one thing is necessary. Mary has chosen the good portion, which will not be taken away from her.'"

— Luke 10:38–42 —

Lord, busyness has enveloped my life, forcing me to count the cost of following You. I am drowning in a sea of priorities. Too many obligations weigh upon me where if I do not stop and rest, I will have a nervous breakdown. I admit that quality time with You is often an afterthought. If I have time, I read my Bible and pray, but that rarely happens because something always comes up or I default into isolation mode and unplug from those around me. I know there is nothing wrong with needing space when I am pushed and pulled daily. Still, when I have time to myself, all I want is to self-medicate my problems rather than look to Your Word for hope and healing.

Trials of life magnify how much I need You. There will always be other things I could be doing, but that does not negate how important prayer and Bible study are to my well-being. I know You took time to have 1-on-1 time with the Father despite the demands people placed upon You, and I need to learn from Your example. Help me discern what I can reduce from my schedule so I am not distracted by busyness but more in tune with Your Spirit. I cannot hear Your voice if I am too busy to listen, so help me make more time for You instead. Amen.

Proceed with Caution

(Carelessness)

*"Be not rash with your mouth, nor let your heart be hasty to utter
a word before God, for God is in heaven and you are on earth.
Therefore let your words be few."*

— *Ecclesiastes 5:2* —

Lord, I am more volatile with my emotions than I should and speak far too freely without guarding my tongue. When a thought enters my mind, it does not take long before I say it. My opinions tend to bypass my conscience and burst forth without wise discretion. I believe honesty is the best policy, but my mouth has gotten me in trouble because I speak too hastily before prayerfully discerning how my words might impact others. People value my opinion and I am thankful for that, but I often fail to think before I speak. I lack a universal filter to ensure what I say is for blessing and not cursing, and it is clearly evident by the wake of destruction I have caused. Why is carelessness such a struggle for me? How can I remedy the problem before I cause more carnage with my words?

King Solomon was right that I should not be hasty in speech but use discernment to calculate the impact of what I say before I say it. There is wisdom in letting my words be few, and I need to heed that advice. Rather than react spontaneously, I am better served pausing before I utter a word so I respond with proper judgment instead of personal opinion. You are never hasty with me, Lord, and I need to apply the same behavior in my speech so I bless others and honor You. Thank You for being so patient with me despite my foolishness. As a Christian, I represent the name of Jesus in this lost world, and I do not want to draw people away from You based on my reckless behavior. Rather, help me be a light to the world of Your love and grace. Amen.

Personal Bias

(Prejudice)

*"There is neither Jew nor Greek, there is neither slave nor free, there is no
male and female, for you are all one in Christ Jesus. And if you are
Christ's, then you are Abraham's offspring, heirs according to promise."*

— Galatians 3:28–29 —

Lord, I tend to look down upon others who do not look or act like me. It is not my intent to hold personal bias, but I segregate myself at times for no apparent reason. I cast judgment based on behavior and outward appearance rather than take time to get to know someone first. People come from all walks of life. The world is a cultural melting pot of relative truths and ideologies, but that does not give me the right to judge others unfairly. You alone are the final moral authority in this world, and I need to step off my high horse and embrace humility. I tend to think more highly of myself than I ought and my behavior is drawing people away from Jesus. Please forgive my foolishness. I want to be a righteous example for Your kingdom, but I seem to be doing more harm than good.

Your Word reminds me that there is a distinct difference between my physical and spiritual identity. You created me in Your own image. I am fearfully and wonderfully made. However, I am born into sin and must decide whether to follow You or choose a different path toward destruction. I do not want to see others separated from Your presence, but I know that in order to communicate Your message of salvation to a lost world, I must die to personal bias and love others like Jesus would. Judgment is not my cross to bear but Yours, and I repent of taking ownership over that right for far too long. I once was lost but now am found, so help me share my testimony of faith with others so they too may come to saving faith in Jesus Christ. Amen.

Take Heart

(Discouragement)

"I have said these things to you, that in me you may have peace.
In the world you will have tribulation.
But take heart; I have overcome the world."

— John 16:33 —

Lord, my heart is so discouraged. When I look around, I see chaos and confusion. Disease and famine are widespread. War rages at home and abroad. Religious freedoms are persecuted and immorality is rampant. Inflation continues to climb and I am struggling to make ends meet. I cannot hide my frustration anymore. My sanity is failing and hope in the joy of tomorrow feels like a mirage. I know that Your Word exhorts me to take courage, but I cannot see the forest through the trees right now. My mind is too focused on the many trials before me to see Your hand at work. I trust You have a plan and purpose for my life, but I cannot understand how at the moment. I am simply too tired and worn out from weathering the storm to gaze upon the sun rising just beyond the horizon.

Even still, my hope is in You alone. No matter how difficult trials may be, I will not surrender and allow discouragement to guide my path. Instead, I will trust Your Spirit and the power of Your Word to illuminate truth amid chaos and hope amongst despair. Satan's army will not prevail against me, for You sit upon the throne. Victory has already been won through the cross of Calvary, so I have nothing to fear. Anxiety holds no power in Your presence, for You are the true source of peace in this world. I praise You for overcoming darkness by the blood of Jesus who died for my sins. Thus, help me keep my eyes fixed on You so I am not tempted to yield to discouragement but rather trust Your sovereign will for my life. Amen.

Embittered Soul

(Bitterness)

*"When my soul was embittered, when I was pricked in heart,
I was brutish and ignorant; I was like a beast toward you."*

— Psalm 73:21–22 —

Lord, my blood boils with resentment for many wrongs committed against me. My flesh longs for vigilante justice where I may enact vengeance for retribution long overdue. I see no wrong taking it upon myself to make amends for the past. My mind has long been haunted by dark memories. I cannot seem to escape the terror of the night. My heart grows faint waiting on Your hand of justice to defend my honor and fall upon the wicked. Am I not justified to hold even the slightest taste of bitterness on my tongue? Why should I freely forgive when my assailers make no effort to repent and seek restitution? I do not wish to drink from this cup of poison, but I am weary of waiting for peace to calm my embittered soul. Letting go of the past should be easy, but yesterday's sins are fresh in my mind and I long to escape their prison.

Understanding begins with the truth of Your Word and Psalm 73 brings conviction to my heart. For far too long, a thirst for blood has clouded my judgment and made me a beast of the field. I am ashamed of how lost I have become, consumed by anger and hell-bent on inflicting an "eye for an eye" and "tooth for a tooth." Retaliation is not Your will for my life, though. Instead, You call me to love my enemies and pray for those who persecute me. I struggle knowing how to bring that to fruition outside of putting complete faith and trust in the Spirit to protect my heart and guide my actions. Please forgive me for losing perspective that I am a sinner and worthy of death outside of a saving relationship with Jesus. Help me lay my bitterness down at the foot of the cross so I may find peace for my troubled soul. Amen.

Lacking Nothing

(Pessimism)

*"For the LORD your God has blessed you in all the work of your hands.
He knows you're going through this great wilderness. These forty years
the LORD your God has been with you. You have lacked nothing."*

— Deuteronomy 2:7 —

Lord, my perspective is glass-half-empty right now. As much as I wish I could be optimistic, I am consumed by negative attitudes. There is no light at the end of the tunnel. This wilderness is never-ending and I see no point going any further. How can there be hope in this barren wasteland? I am mocked by scavengers encircling my head, seeking to devour my flesh. Each day feels the same despite my best effort to find a silver-lining in trials. In some sense, I can relate to Your people of old who wandered forty years in the wilderness. I can only imagine the enormity of their frustration and fatigue eating manna daily and wandering aimlessly. Yet in some way, I know their struggle all too well because I fail to count my blessings each day.

I often forget to remind myself that Your provision is perfect. I lack nothing because You sovereignly take care of my needs. I tend to focus only on my wants and desires, but You promise nothing of the kind. Instead, You instruct me to trust Your Spirit and not concern myself with fear, doubt, and worry. Satan would have me believe You are intentionally withholding blessings from me because I am unworthy of receiving them. He wants me to assume that sin has severed our relationship to the point where I am on my own and must fend for myself. That is merely a lie, though, for I know the plans You have for me are beneficial. Help me count my blessings daily and give thanks, even in my trials, for my hope is found in You no matter what the future might bring. Amen.

Deeply Offended
(Personal Offense)

*"A brother offended is more unyielding than a strong city,
and quarreling is like the bars of a castle."*

— Proverbs 18:19 —

Lord, I tend to think of myself as easy going. I try to let things roll off my shoulders and not take life too seriously. I give others the benefit of the doubt because that is how I prefer to be treated, but the same sentiment is not being reciprocated. I do not wish to hold a grudge against my loved ones, but words cut deep and I cannot shake feeling attacked and insulted. I committed no offense, so why am I on the receiving end of wrath and judgment? It is not fair! A deep wedge has now come between us and I see no path towards reconciliation unless You intervene and bring conviction to their heart. I do not want tension to fester, but anger is consuming my mind and I want nothing more than to tell them how I feel without a care in the world for the damage I may cause in return.

How foolish I must be to believe I am justified acting upon sinful anger. I can hear Satan laughing in the distance, knowing how often I fall prey to deception. The enemy's desire is to bait me into thinking everyone else is my enemy. Sadly, he has succeeded more often than not in doing so. I do not wish to quarrel with anyone, especially those to which I am close. Time is too short to hold grudges and ill-will, no matter how justified I may be feeling offended. That is why You exhort me to love and forgive so my conscience may be clear when I stand before You on judgment day. No peace exists outside the confines of Your grace and mercy. As such, please help me to extend the same blessing to others so that souls may be won for Your kingdom based on my application of Scripture. Amen.

The Wise Fool

(Foolishness)

"Let no one deceive himself. If anyone among you thinks that he is wise in this age, let him become a fool that he may become wise."

— 1 Corinthians 3:18 —

Lord, it no surprise I have made countless bad decisions through-out my lifetime. As hard as I try, I continue to fall into the same trap and sin against You. Behavior modification is futile, so what can I do to resist temptation and live for righteousness? Your Word affirms that **"folly is bound up in the heart of a child, but the rod of discipline drives it far from him" (Proverbs 22:15)**. What level of discipline is necessary to break my pride once and for all? I have no interest making the same mistakes but expecting different outcomes. That is the definition of insanity and I refuse to be a fool any longer. What intrigues me is that I must become a fool to become wise. That does not make sense to me, but I do see how self-deception can lead me to believe I am farther along in my faith journey than reality proves.

Wisdom from above is pure and holy, and I long to bathe in those healing waters. The rollercoaster of foolishness I have been on has only led me back to when I first began. I believe that is what Paul meant to convey—foolishness leads to wisdom because it provides ample opportunity for me to learn from my poor choices. If I think I know better, I have already lost, because I cannot become wise apart from the power of Your Word. Please forgive me for not spending time in Scripture like I should. Studying the Bible does not come naturally to me, but I know it is my spiritual nourishment to survive the dangers of this world. As such, help me discipline my mind to prioritize quality time in prayer so Your Spirit can illuminate truth in my heart. I long to live for righteousness and turn from foolish behavior, Lord. Amen.

Personal Setback
(Disappointment)

"And we know that for those who love God all things work together for good, for those who are called according to his purpose."

— Romans 8:28 —

Lord, there are times where I could just take it or leave it. In those instances, I have no demands on the future. Whatever happens is inconsequential because it has no bearing on my attitude or temperament. However, there are aspects of my life which cause undue stress, fear, and anxiety. They hinge upon assumptions and expectations and inevitably lead me to frustration and disappointment. Those moments test the fabric of my being and whether I believe the inerrancy of Your Word. I cannot read Romans 8:28 and not face the fact that I have a faith problem. I hear what You are saying, but my heart is caught in a spider's web of despair, and the enemy will not release me from its deadly snare. All I can do is cry out to You for salvation and trust that Your will for my life is far greater than I can fathom.

Trials have a way of plunging my heart into hopelessness. It is all a matter of faith and whether my hope is found in You or the things of this world for salvation. For years, I thought I could strongarm my way through life devoid of help. Now, I realize how important it is to exchange my yoke of slavery for Your gift of grace. Disappointment has been a dysfunctional security blanket I've used to justify my poor attitude. I regret allowing the enemy to steal my joy and distract me from living in peace and contentment. I have been so consumed with negative thoughts that I have forgotten to count my blessings daily. Please forgive me for taking Your patience for granted. Despite my doubt, You love me without exception and draw me into Your presence with open arms. I owe everything I am to You, Lord. Amen.

Humble Thyself
(Pride)

"Let the lowly brother boast in his exaltation, and the rich in his humiliation, because like a flower of the grass he will pass away."

— *James 1:9–10* —

Lord, I am dangerously close to self-destruction. Pride is eating at my flesh and I need Your divine intervention to rescue my soul. Humility does not come naturally to me. I struggle giving thanks in trials and joyfully singing praises amid adversity. I would much rather sit high upon the mountaintop than suffer deep in the valley. Even still, I am beginning to understand that reverent humiliation is the linchpin of my identity in Christ. You call me to not merely embrace the idea of humiliation but rather the obedient act of humbling myself before others. Humility is not theory but application, and I fall woefully short of measuring up to Your standard of righteousness. I cannot seem to relinquish my prideful tendencies, no matter how hard I try, and my inability to humble myself is drawing me further away from You.

I am convicted by the power of Your Word, for my heart is exposed to the weight of sin's conviction. I hear Your truth ringing in my ears, reminding me of how foolish I have been to exalt in my self-deception. I am reminded, **"Can a man carry fire next to his chest and his clothes not be burned? Or can one walk on hot coals and his feet not be scorched?" (Proverbs 6:27–28)**. Regrettably, I lean upon my own understanding far too often and it is sealing my fate apart from Your presence. Break me of my pride and create a new spirit within me which longs to do Your will. I am nothing without You, Lord, and my pride demonstrates how desperately I need Your grace and mercy. Humiliate me as only You can and redeem me from the stronghold of hell, so I may be useful for Your kingdom's purpose. Amen.

Fork in the Road

(Discernment)

"So when the woman saw that the tree was good for food, and that it was a delight to the eyes, and that the tree was to be desired to make one wise, she took of its fruit and ate, and she also gave some to her husband who was with her, and he ate. Then the eyes of both were opened, and they knew that they were naked. And they sewed fig leaves together and made themselves loincloths."

— *Genesis 3:6–7* —

Lord, I have sinned against You. I have no justification. No alibi. I chose to reject the truth of Your Word and I am languishing in regret for things I have done. Like Eve, I know what Your Word says to guard my heart from the enemy's schemes and lead me towards righteousness. You gave me a conscience to wisely discern right from wrong, but I struggle trusting Your Spirit. I've allowed doubt to cloud my judgment, and now I wallow in ashes of lament for my sins. I am no better than Adam, either, for my naïve trust in the judgment of others has supplanted complete reliance upon Your Word for wisdom.

How did I become so susceptible to doubt? Why would I allow the enemy to bait me into disbelieving Your Word? Regret is my constant companion. I cannot take back the poor decisions I have made. I can only learn from the consequences of my actions and set my gaze upon greener pastures where grace and mercy are found. I am amazed by Your love for me. Despite my guilt and shame, You cleanse my wounds and bind them with oil. My heart longs for the opportunity to learn from foolishness and make better decisions which glorify You. Help me to never doubt the truth of Your Word but hold fast to it, no matter the cost. I am alive in Christ despite my scars and humbly thank You for the gift of second chances. Amen.

Vengeance is Mine

(Vengeance)

"Beloved, never avenge yourselves, but leave it to the wrath of God, for it is written, 'Vengeance is mine, I will repay, says the Lord.'"

— Romans 12:19 —

Lord, why am I so consumed with a desire to return evil for evil? What right do I have to harbor bitterness against anyone when I am certainly no better? I grievously sin against You every day, yet You do not cast me into the pit of hell. Despite my blatant disregard for the absolute truth of Your Word, I am forgiven and redeemed. It all makes holding onto a grudge impossible to bear. I cannot stomach knowing that what others have done to me pales in comparison to the sacrifice You made on the cross of Calvary. I am torn inside. My flesh longs for retribution—to carry out judgment and execute wrath against those who have hurt me. I do not understand why letting go is so difficult. Forgiveness should be easy, but it is the hardest sacrifice to make because it forces me to trust Your timing and judgment to bring full accountability to fruition.

That is why I cannot sit and wait for judgment to come upon my enemies. Rather, I must learn to love and forgive because Jesus has saved me. Not to say letting go is easy, but I trust Your will be done. Help me to not interfere in Your sovereign plans, Lord. I cannot see what the future holds. For all I know, You may be drawing my oppressors to repentance as a result of my suffering. Your ways are far greater than I can fathom, and You always have my best interest in mind when I cannot see it. Teach me to resist wanting revenge, knowing that bitterness and hostility only draw me further away from Your presence. Instead, help me to love those who persecute me, for You are in full control and I trust Your will for my life. Amen.

Don't You Worry

(Worry)

*"And do not seek what you are to eat and what you are to drink,
nor be worried. For all the nations of the world seek after these things,
and your Father knows that you need them."*

— *Luke 12:29–30* —

Lord, I am so worried that I cannot think straight. Time is running out and my day of reckoning fast approaches. I can feel anxiety beginning to rise deep inside me. How will I make it through this trial? What will the future hold? Will I face this disaster all alone? When can I expect this storm to pass and my life return to normal? Where will I turn if I cannot make ends meet? Why must I endure hardship in this manner? Truly, a million hypothetical questions are flooding my mind. What if life does not go as expected or things turn for the worst? I have no assurance that what awaits me on the other side of the horizon will be for my benefit, so how do I trust Your will for my life, regardless of the outcome?

Your Word seems too good to be true sometimes. Trust Jesus and believe. Oh, if it were only that easy! I lament the immense amount of hours I have wasted away exhausting every possible outcome in my brain. You probably shake Your head watching me worry myself into a panic. My psyche is exhausted to say the least. How much longer can I keep my sanity? Even still, You lull my head to sleep and bring peace to my aching body. I am thankful for peace and quiet. Help me cast my cares upon You so I am not burdened by an unpredictable future but content to live for the present. You have met every need of mine throughout my life. Why I doubt that You will do it again is a mystery. Increase my faith, Lord, so I may claim victory before the battle begins and give You all the glory and praise You deserve. Amen.

Healing Waters
(Agony)

*"Heal me, O LORD, and I shall be healed; save me,
and I shall be saved, for you are my praise."*

— Jeremiah 17:14 —

Lord, You know where I sit and where I stand. You are my shield and comfort when trials overwhelm my soul. I come to You now because I am tired and weary. Pain has plagued me for many years and I have grown accustomed to suffering. I know that I live in a fallen world and life will never be easy, but I pray You would heal me from my affliction and create in me a clean heart, mind, and soul. Some trials in life are self-inflicted; others bear no consequence of my own doing. Regardless, the enemy wants me to blame You for my lot in life. I am certainly convinced that what does not break me will only make me stronger, but I am struggling to see the light at the end of the tunnel. What am I missing and how can I shift my perspective to count my blessings rather than view trials as a burden?

Life is all about choices. I can choose to view my agony as a blessing or a curse. It is impossible to blame You, though, because I can see the silver-lining of Your grace and mercy. Your Spirit reminds me that my identity is not based upon the difficult trials I face, but on the blood of Christ who died to set me free. Help me to remember that. I can easily get lost in the wilderness of my mind and allow the enemy to plant seeds of bitterness in my heart. I know that expecting specific outcomes only paints You into a corner, and I want to avoid that trap. You are sovereign and I am not, so help me trust that the reasons for my calamities will be revealed in Your way and time. Blessings await those who trust in the Lord, and I will hold fast to the promise of Your Word all the days of my life. Amen.

Victory in Jesus
(Affliction)

*"For everyone who has been born of God overcomes the world.
And this is the victory that has overcome the world—our faith.
Who is it that overcomes the world except the one
who believes that Jesus is the Son of God?"*

— 1 John 5:4–5 —

Lord, no matter what trials come my way, I am encouraged to know You are with me in the fire. When I accepted Jesus as my personal Lord and Savior, I knew that life would continue to test my patience. I was not naïve to assume that life would be easy. Quite the contrary! In fact, I expected Satan to increase his attacks against me with newfound ferocity. Indeed, my faith has been pushed to the brink of late. Trials have tempted me to question why I am being afflicted with pain and suffering, doubt, and worry. It seems the road to sanctification is steep and winding, making it extremely difficult to gather my wits about me and reach the mountaintop with daylight to spare. I certainly trust Your sovereign will for my life, but I am tired and weary from the journey.

Despite my affliction, Your Word comforts my aching soul. I am not crushed, driven to despair, forsaken, or destroyed by trials but set free to live for righteousness. It is too easy to identify myself by the burdens I carry as they can be a dysfunctional security blanket I wear to garner sympathy from others. You do not want me to wallow in self-pity, though, but to rise from the ashes and see the beauty of Your creation. You work all things together for my good and I praise You for being so gracious to me. I do not deserve the many blessings You provide when my faith wanders off course, but I humbly thank You for loving me when my heart grows weary. I am victorious because of Your precious blood and will sing Your praises forevermore. Amen.

Vindication is Mine

(False Accusation)

*"Vindicate me, O LORD, for I have walked in my integrity,
and I have trusted in the LORD without wavering.
Prove me, O LORD, and try me; test my heart and my mind. For your
steadfast love is before my eyes, and I walk in your faithfulness."*

— Psalm 26:1–3 —

Lord, I have been falsely accused. I am tired of being looked down upon by others. What I'm being judged for is unfair. I committed no crime. I am not harboring guilt or being dishonest to avoid punishment. I did nothing wrong! Even still, I am apparently guilty before being proven innocent and condemned rather than pardoned. Why do others seek retribution against me? Their thirst for vengeance makes no sense. If I have unknowingly sinned, help me recognize the error of my ways and accept complete responsibility for my actions. I am not perfect and can be blind to my own blindness at times. However, if I am innocent in Your eyes, please let the truth be known so my name is protected from slander.

Judgment is Yours, of course, for You are my redeemer. I confidently stand before You with a clear conscience knowing the victory is won. I have walked in integrity and held firm to the validity of Your Word. Help me remain steadfast in my pursuit of righteousness. No matter what others may say, I will not be swayed from trusting Your sovereignty because I answer to You alone. Many have sought to condemn me for defending Your Word, but I count it an honor and privilege to be persecuted for Your name. I praise You for being faithful in my hour of need. Make me an instrument of Your peace in the face of adversity. I am vindicated because You found me innocent of wrongdoing. Thank You for Your unending grace and mercy. Amen.

Melancholy Mood
(Gloom)

*"Why are you cast down, O my soul, and why are you in turmoil
within me? Hope in God; for I shall again praise him,
my salvation and my God."*

— Psalm 42:5 —

Lord, my emotions are all over the board. I feel sad and depressed. My heart grieves with tears amidst brokenness. I cannot seem to shake these thoughts of despair. They smother me to the point where I find it difficult to breathe. I do not understand why my mind is so easily drawn to negativity and pessimism, but this season of life I am in has me wrought with fear, doubt, and worry. My glass is far from being half-empty. It has been dry and barren for quite some time with no end in sight. All I want is to sleep and bury my thoughts deep within the shadows of my mind so I may never find them again. Why is my soul so downcast? I know the promises of Your Word are true, but I am struggling to see light at the end of the tunnel. What am I missing?

Spiritual warfare is intense for me these days. The more I lean into Your Word for hope, the enemy snatches my joy away, leaving me frustrated and heartbroken. It is difficult to maintain a positive attitude when trials continue to push my mind to the brink of insanity. Yet, in my darkest hours, You bring relief through the power of Your Spirit within me. I am reminded of Your faithfulness—how You once pulled me out of depths of my despair and will do it again, if necessary. You are so good to me, Lord, despite my lack of faith in Your sovereignty. Help me trust that Your plan and purpose for my life far exceeds what I can fathom at this point. I do not need to reach the mountaintop to look back and see Your hand at work in my life. I know You are faithful, and I praise You for loving me in my darkest hours. Amen.

Content with Weakness

(Weakness)

"For the sake of Christ, then, I am content with weaknesses,
insults, hardships, persecutions, and calamities.
For when I am weak, then I am strong."

— 2 Corinthians 12:10 —

Lord, I wish contentment were easy to attain! I can only imagine what my life would look like if I had all I needed to be happy. The truth of the matter is I already do. I just fail to count my blessings. I am far too concerned with what I lack to stop and thank You for all You have done for me. However, I am struggling to understand why I am being afflicted. Why must I be insulted by others, persecuted for my faith, and overwhelmed by hardships? I look around and see others who defiantly blaspheme Your name prospering in this world without a care or concern. Meanwhile, I am fighting to keep my sanity and not fold under the weight of trials which seem to compound over time. Is it not too much to ask You for a bit of relief?

Your Word reminds me that trials are not punishments but golden opportunities to grow closer to You. If I were successful from the world's lofty standards, I would likely be spiritually bankrupt because prosperity is not measured by monetary wealth but contentment. It is the secret of life which You have made abundantly clear to me over the years. Truly, I can rest peacefully because Christ is glorified when I stand in the face of adversity and affliction and praise You for it. I cannot say that I always understand why I am made to suffer, but I know that personal weakness keeps me dependent upon You, to which I am eternally grateful. Keep my eyes focused on the silver-lining of Your grace interwoven throughout the fabric of my life, so I can be happy and content regardless of my circumstances. Amen.

Growing Resentment
(Resentment)

"But he answered his father, 'Look, these many years I have served you,
and I never disobeyed your command, yet you never gave me
a young goat, that I might celebrate with my friends.
But when this son of yours came, who has devoured your property
with prostitutes, you killed the fattened calf for him!'"

— Luke 15:29–30 —

Lord, when I read the Parable of the Prodigal Son, I empathize with the older brother's thoughts and feelings. I understand his anger because I have felt it too during seasons of my life. I try to live for righteousness and follow Your commands, yet it seems as if I am left emptyhanded more often than not. Why do those who want nothing to do with You prosper while I struggle to make ends meet? Are there not any blessings left for me to enjoy? Am I made to grit and bear the yoke of expectations while others seem to have none? I know that my attitude is poor and I repent of complaining about Your provision. I have everything I need and give thanks to You for never abandoning me in my hour of need. Why am I harboring feelings of resentment, though, when I have nothing to be bitter about, all things considered?

If You gave me what I deserve, I would have been thrown into the pit of hell for my sins against You. I am no better than my neighbor. We are both subject to eternal judgment, yet I need to be reminded that You died for me just as much as the prodigal who squandered his inheritance for the pleasures of this world. I have no right to judge the actions of others or embitter my soul against the lost. Resentment is not Your will for life. Therefore, help me die to selfish attitudes and give thanks when other prodigals return home in humble repentance to Your saving grace. Amen.

Abandoned Love

(Rebellion)

*"But I have this against you, that you have abandoned the love you had
at first. Remember therefore from where you have fallen; repent and do
the works you did at first. If not, I will come to you and remove
your lampstand from its place, unless you repent."*

— *Revelation 2:4–5* —

Lord, Your Word cuts like a knife deep within my soul. You accuse me of abandoning my love for You and my neighbor, but I fail to understand why. What have I done? Why is Your anger kindled against me? I will admit I can be spiritually blind to my own blindness, but my intent is to honor You in everything I say and do. Help me examine my thoughts and behavior from Your perspective so I may guard my heart from thinking more highly of myself than I ought. You provide incredible clarity when I pray for wisdom and understanding, and I need to recognize the error of my ways to avoid leading others astray in their faith journey. I have somehow lost my sense of direction and need You to illuminate the path of righteousness so I may walk in it.

When I look back to where my spiritual rebirth began, I can see how the fire which once burned bright has faded over time. My hunger to know You and read Your Word has waned into a shell of its former self. I no longer prioritize You first in my day, making sure we spend quality time together. Rather, I am too consumed with busyness and the pleasures of this world to discipline my mind and keep my priorities straight. I have become too self-consumed and, yes, my love for You and my neighbor have gone by the wayside. Please forgive me. I never intended to drift aimlessly in my faith and take Your love, grace, and mercy for granted. Give me a renewed desire to rekindle my love for You and those You place in my path each day. Amen.

Under Siege

(Oppression)

"Be gracious to me, O God, for man tramples on me;
all day long an attacker oppresses me; my enemies trample on me
all day long, for many attack me proudly."

— Psalm 56:1–2 —

Lord, why do others hate me so much? When I look in the mirror, all I see are bruises. Some visible. Others well beneath the surface. I would feel better if I was simply dealing with scars, but these wounds will not go away. They only reappear each time Satan unleashes a new attack to destroy me permanently. I am reminded that this world is not my home. I understand it because everywhere I turn, I come face to face with persecution. My lifestyle does not fit the cultural norm. I seek to live under the authority of Your Word and this world is vehemently at war with Your Spirit. If there was a season of reprieve from torment, I could endure suffering more easily. However, the enemy has been relentless in his attack and I am struggling to survive.

I covet Your grace like an oasis amid desert heat. My mind can only imagine how glorious it will be to spend eternity with You in heaven one day. No more sickness. No more pain. No more war within my mind. When that day comes, the enemy will be languishing in agony, not me. I will walk along streets of gold and praise the mighty name of Jesus, my Savior. Even so, You call me to endure hatred on behalf of Your Son who died in my place. Through His blood, I am rescued and redeemed. I have no need to fear the terror of the night because You are my shelter, the rock in whom I trust. Joy comes to those who lean not on their own understanding but the truth of Your Word for hope and healing. Help me to remain true to accomplish Your will each day, no matter how difficult the road may be to tread. Amen.

Paralyzed by Terror
(Judgment)

*"The king mourns, the prince is wrapped in despair, and the hands
of the people of the land are paralyzed by terror. According to their way
I will do to them, and according to their judgments I will judge them,
and they shall know that I am the LORD."*

— Ezekiel 7:27 —

Lord, my soul is overrun with regret, for I am a sinner in Your holy and righteous hands. You demand justice—that sin be atoned for, and I am destined for eternal separation from You if I do not repent of my transgressions and reconcile with others. The scales of justice have not weighed in my favor. I wouldn't expect them to considering how I pridefully disregarded Your warnings and blazed my own trail in the wilderness. Now, I stand before You parched and empty in this barren wasteland, yearning for a mere drop of water from Your Word. Truly, my soul is paralyzed by terror. Like a tidal wave of destruction, despair has crushed me under its limitless weight, and I fear that I may never see the light of day again. What shall I do?

Despite the enormity of judgment before me, I am not hopeless. I do not assume You have abandoned me either. Your judgment against sin is just and necessary, but the blood of Jesus covers my iniquities to which I am eternally grateful. Thank You for Your love and wrath. They are equal parts of Your righteous character and I praise You that You do not let me wallow in sin. Rather, You love me enough to save me from self-destruction and the consequences of living independently from You. I can never repay You for all You have done for me. Satan holds no power over me because You stood in my place and accepted the death I deserved. As such, I will glorify You all the days of my life because You alone are worthy of honor and praise. Amen.

Green with Envy

(Envy)

"Truly God is good to Israel, to those who are pure in heart. But as for me, my feet had almost stumbled, my steps had nearly slipped. For I was envious of the arrogant when I saw the prosperity of the wicked."

— *Psalm 73:1–3* —

Lord, Scripture warns me not to covet my neighbor's possessions, yet I struggle reconciling how those who are arrogant prosper. The wicked boldly shake their fist in Your face and boast of their good fortune as if their accomplishments are self-made rather than given by You. How can I sit idle and watch them revel in their arrogance? They are intoxicated under the influence of Satan's deadly poison. They assume their prosperity is a sign of righteousness, but that is not true. It angers me to watch them mock Your grace as if they had anything to do with their good fortune. All blessings come from You, even trials which test the depth and breadth of my faith. Why then must I struggle with hunger and thirst while the wicked lavishly fill their bellies with choice fruits and drink to their heart's content?

Please forgive my envious soul. Worldly pleasures are not a sign of spiritual prosperity but a slippery slope towards gluttony. Happiness is not based upon the quantity of my possessions but the attitude of my heart and appreciation for all You have given me. Help me count my blessings and give thanks each day for all You have blessed me with. My salvation alone is reason enough to never need anything more to achieve contentment. Nevertheless, You shower me with love and affection which I do not deserve, all because You want what is best for my life. Help me to never forget Your love. As for the wicked, may they come to repentance and recognize the error of their ways. For all good things come from above, and You alone are the source. Amen.

High and Mighty

(Conceit)

"For by the grace given to me I say to everyone among you not to think of himself more highly than he ought to think, but to think with sober judgment, each according to the measure of faith that God has assigned."

— Romans 12:3 —

Lord, I am far too arrogant to admit how puffed up I have become. I tend to think of myself as smart, talented, and qualified, but I am quickly learning I know far less than once presumed. Trials of life have humbled me far more than I imagined and it is difficult to come to terms with the fact that I am a shell of my former self. Never before have I felt so inept or undignified. It pains me to ask for help even with the most menial of tasks. People used to ask me for help and advice. Now I am eating humble pie daily. How did life change so quickly? I was once "somebody," but now I feel lost and forgotten. You have knocked me off my high horse, and I fear that I may never have the opportunity to stand again and prove my self-worth.

It pains me to admit that I had it coming, thinking I knew better than You. For years, I relied upon my own strength, knowledge, and ability to get things done. Rarely did I give You credit for the grace You gave me when I least deserved it. I took credit for what You did in and through me, and I deeply regret my foolish ways. Everything I am and all I have been given is solely due to Your abundant grace. I am forever indebted to You for loving me despite my arrogance. Please forgive me for thinking more highly of myself than I ought. I accept the discipline and punishment I deserve for stealing Your glory. Thank You for being patient with me as I work out my salvation with fear and trembling. Your lovingkindness knows no bounds. Help me rejoice in my weaknesses. For when I am weak, then I am made strong. Amen.

Forget Me Not

(Immaturity)

*"But the one who looks into the perfect law, the law of liberty,
and perseveres, being no hearer who forgets but a doer who acts,
he will be blessed in his doing."*

— James 1:25 —

Lord, it seems crazy for someone to look in the mirror, turn away, and then forget what he or she looks like. I struggle reconciling how that is even possible. I know I can get forgetful at times. Fatigue can make me weary where my mind may not be firing on all cylinders, but to forget completely is insane! It only seems feasible if I were legally blind. I could understand where You are coming from if that were the case. Nevertheless, I know that is not what You are warning me about. You are far more concerned about the attitude of my heart and whether I take Your Word serious enough to do what it says. I can honestly say it is far easier to quote Scripture than live it out. I have become very proficient at saying I'm a Christian but often lack physical proof to verify how I live out my faith in word and deed.

Your patience with me is unbelievable and Your ways are so much higher than mine. I doubt that I could continue to show myself grace if I were in Your shoes. Frustration would be immense, yet You refuse to cast me away from Your presence. Instead, You give me countless opportunities to change my ways because Your love is everlasting. I praise You because You have not forgotten me as I have with You. Conviction weighs heavy on my heart, for I know You would never forsake me. Please guard me from hypocrisy so I do not say one thing yet do the exact opposite. My testimony is made possible only because of Jesus, and I never want to lead others astray by not taking my faith serious enough. Amen.

Free Indeed

(Bondage)

"I am the LORD your God, who brought you out of the land of Egypt,
that you should not be their slaves. And I have broken the bars
of your yoke and made you walk erect."

— Leviticus 26:13 —

Lord, all of my life I have been enslaved to sin, shackled in bondage to the prince of darkness. My oppressor is cunning in his rebuke of my identity in Christ. He tempts me to believe that my decision to follow You was disingenuous and fake. Doubt has overwhelmed my heart and caused me to lose hope that You can save me from this pit I now call home. I am exhausted, Lord—weary to the point of collapse. These chains have become an extension of who I am. They cut deep into my flesh and rub my skin raw to the bone with shame and regret. How I can find victory in this barren wasteland is a mystery. I cannot see the sun through the clouds surrounding me, and I fear I never will.

Arise, O Lord, and save my weary soul! Cast me not from Your presence but renew a right spirit with me—a spirit of faith, hope, and trust in the power of Your Word. Release me from these shackles and bind the enemy from enslaving me further. I cannot save myself no matter how hard I try. Help me surrender my life to You. Teach me to not withhold a single ounce of submission, so I may walk humbly in the shadow of my Savior. My identity is safe and secure in the blood of Jesus. I pray I never forget the immeasurable sacrifice You made to set me free. Satan holds no power if I abide in You without reservation. Therefore, help me stand upright in victory, for You have released me from my prison walls and given me new life in Christ. Tomorrow is a new day, and I will proclaim Your glory because You loved me enough to set this captive free for all eternity. Amen.

Decisions, Decisions

(Discernment)

*"See, I am setting before you today a blessing and a curse: the blessing, if
you obey the commandments of the LORD your God, which I command
you today, and the curse, if you do not obey the commandments of the
LORD your God but turn aside from the way that I am commanding
you today, to go after other gods that you have not known."*

— Deuteronomy 11:26–28 —

Lord, I have come upon a fork in the road and do not know which
way I should turn. I know You are with me no matter which path
I take, but I would rather avoid making the wrong choice, if possible.
You lay before me two options which have the ability to change my
life forever: blessing and cursing. It should be easy to distinguish them
but my mind is torn for some reason. I am drawn like a moth to a
flame by worldly pleasures. The promise of satisfaction sounds good
to me, but I know it is only temporary. Not to say I am ungrateful for
Your constant provision, but I am tired of eating manna in the desert.
I crave more, and the enemy is making it easy for me to obey my flesh
and take hold of the forbidden fruit.

Why am I so mentally weak when I know the gate is wide and leads
to destruction? Your Word is choice fruit, yet I am willing to throw it
all away like Esau did for a bowl of soup. Have I truly fallen so far out
of touch with reality that I am willing to trade my birthright for
momentary pleasure? Heaven forbid! You prepare a banquet feast in
the presence of my enemies. Help me to not cast aside Your great
bounty for what the world has to offer. The decisions I ultimately make
stick with me the rest of my life, so give me discernment to choose
wisely. I do not want to be led astray by worldly comforts but instead
remain devout in my decision to trust You no matter what. Amen.

Hot nor Cold

(Indifference)

"I know your works: you are neither cold nor hot. Would that you were either cold or hot! So, because you are lukewarm, and neither hot nor cold, I will spit you out of my mouth."

— Revelation 3:15–16 —

Lord, my journey of faith feels tired and stagnant. When people ask how I am doing, it is easy to say everything is fine, but my heart is plagued by indifference and a lack of care for the world around me. It is difficult to pinpoint where my attitude went awry. I have never been a negative person, but my glass feels half-empty and I cannot seem to free myself from this weight of complacency. I am tired of clocking in-and-out each day with little excitement for what tomorrow may bring. There must be more to life than what this hamster's wheel has to offer. I see no point in doing the same thing over and again but expecting different results. Life does not work that way but I am convinced I am becoming so indifferent toward the world around me that I could care less what happens to me (or anyone else for that matter).

Why have I become so calloused, Lord? My life is not devoid of joy. I have no reason to complain about my lot in life. You have given me abundant life in Christ. How then can I act as if I am indifferent to the needs of others when You sacrificed Yourself for me? Help me die to negativity and count my blessings. Instill a burning desire within me to not be conformed to the pattern of this world but transformed by the renewal of my mind. I long to know more about You. Revive my heart to dive into the pages of Scripture daily. Reveal Your will to me and give me fresh opportunities to share my testimony. I am thankful for the grace You freely provide. Still, help me to not take it for granted but pay it forward to those in need. Amen.

Taking Credit
(Boasting)

"Thus says the LORD: 'Let not the wise man boast in his wisdom, let not the mighty man boast in his might, let not the rich man boast in his riches, but let him who boasts boast in this, that he understands and knows me, that I am the LORD who practices steadfast love, justice, and righteousness in the earth.'"

— Jeremiah 9:23–24 —

Lord, what have I to boast about in this world other than You? The more I consider my gifts, abilities, and accomplishments, the less eager I am to take credit for them. No good exists in me apart from You, and that is abundantly clear when I forget my identity in Christ and glorify myself. I know what it feels like to rot in a pit of filth. When I was lost, my mind clouded with self-exaltation, I sought opportunities to take credit for my achievements. The more I wallowed in pride, the more arrogant I became. Satan had such a stronghold on me that I could not see the error of my ways. My eyes were too fixated on the praises of man. I stole Your glory and felt no remorse propping myself above others to inflate my ego. What a fool I was!

I am humbled by Your patience with me despite my wayward heart. I have certainly learned the art of remaining content in Your sovereign provision. I no longer second guess whether the plans You have for me will be worth my time and energy. I know they will benefit my life far more than I realize. Help me boast all the more in who You are as my Father and King. Let me never forget the immeasurable sacrifice You made to save a wretch like me. I am one life in this vast world of billions, yet You know me by name. What could I ever do to deserve Your love? Your grace is amazing which only makes me thank You all the more as I boast in You alone. Amen.

Idle Sluggard

(Idleness)

"How long will you lie there, O sluggard?
When will you arise from your sleep? A little sleep,
a little slumber, a little folding of the hands to rest, and poverty will come
upon you like a robber, and want like an armed man."

— *Proverbs 6:9–11* —

Lord, sometimes I love doing nothing. I cannot explain it, but I am perfectly content being lazy sometimes and carving out "me time" to recharge my batteries. The problem is I can become so consumed with having time all to myself that I neglect those around me. In other words, idleness has become a stronghold in my life. I long for it, so much so that I lash out in frustration towards anyone who steals my joy. I know that I need rest, but my infatuation with unplugging from the world and sleeping all day is becoming an issue. It is no longer about just recharging my batteries but rejecting all responsibilities in my life to do what I want instead of what others expect from me.

Am I sinning in my desire for momentary reprieve? I don't believe so, but a root of discontentment runs deep within me. My desire for isolation demonstrates that it is not You I seek but the object of my affection. What I yearn for is not wrong, but how I idolize it is where I've gone off the beaten path. Help me see the error of my ways when my infatuation with idleness rears its ugly head. The more I relent to idleness, the more I crave distance from every aspect of my life. I never want to avoid engaging my family or fulfilling duties and obligations, because idleness will only fuel discontentment in other areas of my life. As such, please guard me from the schemes of the enemy and do not grant my idols of affection. Rather, break me from them so I am never tempted to return again. Amen.

Help My Unbelief
(Unbelief)

"And Jesus asked his father, 'How long has this been happening to him?'
And he said, 'From childhood. And it has often cast him into fire
and into water, to destroy him. But if you can do anything, have
compassion on us and help us.' And Jesus said to him, "If you can!"
All things are possible for one who believes.' Immediately the father
of the child cried out and said, 'I believe; help my unbelief!'"

— Mark 9:21–24 —

Lord, I lament the number of times I distrusted Your Word rather than place faith in what I could not see. I fell victim to doubt and questioned whether You really could do something about my plight. I regret needing proof, but my memory is short and I forget how faithful You have been in my life. Who am I to question Your sovereignty and demand explanation? What right do I have to know your plans and purpose ahead of time? The same seed of doubt which tempted Adam and Eve runs through my veins. I am no different than them, because I question the validity of Your Word despite Your clear instructions.

Why is my heart so prone to wander? I do not understand how my faith is so easily undermined by disbelief. You have given me no reason to question Your goodness, yet I default to skepticism when I should hold fast to the assurance of my salvation. Help me filter the lies Satan tempts me to believe by washing my mind with Your absolute truth. Abundant life is found in You, and I will not allow the enemy to steal my joy. What You ask of me is unconditional trust. Therefore, I will tithe the first fruits of my soul's devotion to You, preaching the Gospel to my heart daily and rejecting lies which tempt me to despair. Hope is found in You, Lord, and I will trust Your will for my life no matter what trials inevitably come my way. Amen.

Watch and Pray

(Temptation)

*"Watch and pray that you may not enter into temptation.
The spirit indeed is willing, but the flesh is weak."*

— Matthew 26:41 —

Lord, not a day goes by where I am not tempted to yield to my flesh and satisfy guilty pleasures. Why am I feebleminded? What could this fallen world possibly offer that compares to the joy of my salvation? Satan knows exactly which buttons to push and tempt me. He knows my weaknesses far better than I and has unlimited resources to fulfill my carnal desires. Yet, what He cannot give me, only You can! He cannot assure me eternal joy nor grant me peace and contentment. All he can provide are empty promises which never satisfy but only crave more, for pleasure is nothing but a momentary fix to numb the pain I harbor deep inside. Nevertheless, I often succumb to his lies and assume I am strong enough to say, "No!"

Though I should know better, I often relinquish control and take hold of forbidden fruit I desperately crave. My soul longs to walk away, but I am drawn to sin's inducing aroma like a moth to a flame. Its glow and effervescence intoxicates my senses, yet I know it will ultimately lead to death. Even so, I follow through on my carnal desires only to realize that the oasis I sought was merely a mirage. Why am I so weak, Lord? How is it remotely possible that after all You have done for me, I would yield to my flesh and trade the assurance of my salvation for momentary pleasures? I mourn the depravity of my foolish heart. Help me choose intimacy with You over worldly idols. I am tired of yielding to my desires but long to be free of the chains which have enslaved me far too long. Freedom is found in Your Word alone and I will trust its precepts wholeheartedly and without hesitation. Amen.

Lazy Bones

(Laziness)

"Go to the ant, O sluggard; consider her ways and be wise.
Without having any chief, officer, or ruler, she prepares her bread
in summer and gathers her food in harvest."

— *Proverbs 6:6–8* —

Lord, I tend to be so consumed with today that I fail to consider what lies ahead. I know that tomorrow is not guaranteed, but I cannot act as if planning for the future is meaningless or insignificant. I have responsibilities and people depend on me. To ignore Your call to provide for my family would be foolish, yet I often desire to have my fill rather than ration for the future. Scripture convicts me that I must be diligent to prepare for what lies ahead. For example, the ant is not swayed by momentary pleasures but casts its gaze upon the horizon of changing seasons. It does not need to be reminded of what's at stake but uses self-discipline to plan accordingly. It keeps busy and remains diligent to avoid succumbing to temptation.

I would not consider myself lazy, but I see fruits of idleness in my life. I often lie in bed and think of things I long to accomplish the next day only to be distracted and leave my work unfinished. My mind is overrun with a laundry list of tasks which need immediate attention. I cannot ignore my responsibility, but I often procrastinate what could easily be reconciled today. Why am I so prone to laziness? Why can't I be like an ant and do my job without needing reminders and frequent accountability? I want to be diligent in life and not tossed aimlessly by the pleasures of this world which seek to distract me. Yes, I am allowed time to rest and relax but help me avoid making laziness an idol I use to escape expectations. Help me to also prepare and gather as You see fit and keep my hand on the plow despite difficulties. Amen.

Cowardly Influence
(Cowardice)

"And the officers shall speak further to the people, and say, 'Is there any man who is fearful and fainthearted? Let him go back to his house, lest he make the heart of his fellows melt like his own.'"

— Deuteronomy 20:8 —

Lord, my attitude speaks volumes. I often allow fear to control my actions and it is having a direct impact on those I love. Why am I scared of what might happen? Why does the uncertainty of tomorrow frighten me? My inability to control my emotions is a sign that I fail to trust Your sovereign provision for my life. If I believed no one could harm me when I rest in the shelter of Your wings, I would not be so easily swayed by fear of man. Instead, I see many Goliaths in my life and run away rather than face them. What concerns me most is that my lack of faith has had a ripple effect on others. I know Satan is using me to strike fear into those around me because of my cowardly instincts. He makes me believe the obstacles before me are too large to overcome, and I cave under pressure to presumed destruction.

Yet, when I read Your Word, I am encouraged that David's trust in You is what enabled him to defeat Goliath. It was not by human will or strength that he found victory. Rather, his unwavering faith in Your power is what gave him success that day. Similarly, Joshua and Caleb were not swayed when they were tasked to spy out the Promised Land. Yes, giants roamed there, but they would not be shaken. While others allowed fear to consume them, Joshua and Caleb were resolute that You were more than able to give them victory. Lord, I long for mustard seed faith which is not concerned with the size of the obstacle before me. You are able to move mountains, and I will trust Your Word which reminds me of who I am as Your precious child. Amen.

Despised and Rejected

(Rejection)

"If the world hates you, know that it has hated me before it hated you.
If you were of the world, the world would love you as its own;
but because you are not of the world, but I chose you out of the world,
therefore the world hates you."

— *John 15:18–19* —

Lord, rejection is a dark and lonely road. No matter where life takes me, following You is not easy. At times, I feel like I have a target on my back. Every word I speak is scrutinized to the point where my enemies are waiting for me to fail. They want to prove that I am nothing but a religious hypocrite. I am certainly not perfect. I make bad decisions and sin like everyone else, but how can I avoid hypocrisy? I do not want to be a stumbling block for others to hear what You have to say. Rather, I want to lead them toward Your unending grace, but enemies continue to tear me down. They hurl insults and condemn me as being judgmental and unloving. That is not my intent, though, for only You are righteous to judge. I am just trying to live as best I can!

Your Word reminds me that I am never alone despite persecution. You know better than anyone what it means to be reviled for standing upon moral high ground. No matter what suffering or oppression I face this side of heaven, I will not deny my faith. I will not cower to Satan's schemes nor allow fear to overwhelm my heart. Rather, I will trust my Savior who died to set me free. You never promised a life of ease and comfort, but I repent of assuming that life should be simple. It is clear that the road You have me on is narrow indeed, but it is the path to heaven and I will not seek another way. You brought me out of darkness and into the light of Your grace. Come what may, I will not yield to the enemy despite being rejected by man. Amen.

Greedy Desire
(Greed)

*"But those who desire to be rich fall into temptation, into a snare,
into many senseless and harmful desires that plunge people into ruin
and destruction. For the love of money is a root of all kinds of evils.
It is through this craving that some have wandered away from
the faith and pierced themselves with many pangs."*

— *1 Timothy 6:9–10* —

Lord, the desire for more can be insatiable at times. Power, money, and worldly pleasures all appeal to my senses. I know they will never satisfy because I cannot take them with me when I die. All that matters is whether I have accepted Your gift of salvation. Why then am I so consumed by my flesh? Greed has brought nothing but pain and misery to my life, yet I long for more. Like a dog returns to its vomit, I continue to arrive at an empty well expecting to find water. I am consumed by the allure of an oasis in the distance, yet it is only a mirage. I can almost hear the enemy laughing when I assume this world has anything to truly quench my insatiable thirst.

Whether I have a little or a lot, none of it ultimately matters. The same greedy hunger exists if my heart is bent on needing excess to feel complete. The sad truth is wanting more only leaves me empty inside. No pleasure can fill my cup to the point where I am truly satisfied, for lasting joy and contentment are found in You alone. How then can I find freedom from greed? Please help me avoid this trap of discontentment with Your provision. I lack nothing to survive this world, so keep me joyful amid seasons where I am discontent and tired of grinding my way through life. Trials are nothing more than an opportunity to count my blessings, and I want to praise You with a full heart which appreciates all You have graciously given to me. Amen.

Hateful Poison

(Hate)

*"If anyone says, "I love God," and hates his brother, he is a liar;
for he who does not love his brother whom he has seen
cannot love God whom he has not seen."*

— *1 John 4:20* —

Lord, my heart feels dark and cold. A deep fog weighs heavy upon my mind, longing for retribution against another. This hateful cup of poison held tightly within my grasp is destroying me from within. I do not know how to set it down and walk away. I know that hate is a powerful word I should not use lightly. Rather, it is a stark reminder that my emotions have spiraled out of control. The winding road of life is wrought with sharp turns and steep drop-offs, and hate compels me to take each curve at breakneck speed. I feel lost without a compass to guide me home. I am trapped in a dark room of regret for wishing ill-will against my neighbor. How did I get here and why can I not seem to find a way out of this maze of hate?

It goes without saying that my heart is far from You when it is consumed with hatred. I cannot wish ill will against another yet rest assured that my prayers reach Your ears. I am a fool to believe I can serve two masters. Help me cast my anger and bitterness into the fires of Your grace. Give me strength to love my neighbor instead of wallowing in hate. The more I yield to temptation, the further I drift from You. I want to live in peace—free from the bondage of past memories which enslave me. Help me lay down my desire for revenge and retribution at the foot of Your cross. Let it die there for all eternity! I am renewed by the grace of Your Spirit when I forgive others, so grant me courage to quickly seek reconciliation. I do not want to harbor any semblance of hatred in my heart but rather love my neighbor as myself. Amen.

Thorn in the Flesh

(Torment)

*"So to keep me from becoming conceited because of the surpassing greatness
of the revelations, a thorn was given me in the flesh, a messenger
of Satan to harass me, to keep me from becoming conceited."*

— *2 Corinthians 12:7* —

Lord, not a day goes by where I am unaware of Satan's presence in my life. I can feel his deadly stare bearing down upon me, waiting for the opportune moment to attack. His endless resources bait me into sin, and I am afraid that I will not be able to withstand his arrows of temptation much longer. Even still, I know Your Spirit fights on my behalf, waging war against the legions of demonic forces seeking to destroy my heart and mind. You have never abandoned me in my hour of need, yet I often turn away from the Spirit's conviction and choose what I assume is a better path. Please forgive my naïve foolishness, Lord, for You are longsuffering and forever patient with me when I least deserve it.

I struggle understanding why I am made to suffer. What benefit does this thorn in my flesh serve when it steals the joy of my salvation and tempts me to blame You for my anguish? I can hardly focus my attention on the plans You have for me when all I feel is continuous torment. Even so, Your Word reminds me that the power of Christ is perfected in my weakness (2 Cor. 12:9), and for that I rejoice. Time has weathered my body with aches and pain, but I know You are my source of strength. The sins of my past have left permanent scars as reminders of foolish days long past. Still, I praise You all the more for pulling me out of the darkness and into the light of Your truth. Give me strength to praise You amid suffering as You refine my character into the image of Your precious Son. Amen.

Stubborn as a Mule

(Stubbornness)

*"Circumcise therefore the foreskin of your heart and be no longer stubborn.
For the LORD your God is God of gods and Lord of lords, the great,
the mighty, and the awesome God, who is not partial and takes no bribe."*

— Deuteronomy 10:16–17 —

Lord, I am as stubborn as a mule! Please hear my cries and forgive my repentant soul. For far too long, I have hardened my heart against the truth of Your Word. Rather than bend my personal will to the power of Scripture, I have leaned on my own understanding and now face the consequences of my actions. I certainly know better. Alas, I have chosen poorly! Why am I bent on getting my own way rather than relinquishing control to You? Please help me surrender my pride and not yield to the enemy's schemes which tempt me to hold my ground against You. I am quick to sit and refuse to stand because I think I know better. However, in my arrogance, I only prove how immature I am to disobey Your authority.

My stubborn pride is a bottleneck in our relationship. I must repent of my wicked attitude and learn to walk in obedience. As much as I hate to admit it, I am not far removed from the sins of my past which hold my heart captive to self-preservation rather than submission to Your will. It is embarrassing to believe human intellect and personal experience are superior to Your omniscience. What a fool I am to taunt You in naïve ignorance! You are sovereign over all creation. Help me know my place in Your holy kingdom and listen to Your Spirit's voice. I long to obey Your Word without hesitation, but I need childlike faith to not question authority. Stubbornness is not an attribute I wish to continue, so give me wisdom to lay it down at the foot of Your cross and trust Your will forevermore. Amen.

Harsh Words

(Harshness)

"A soft answer turns away wrath, but a harsh word stirs up anger.
The tongue of the wise commends knowledge,
but the mouths of fools pour out folly."

— *Proverbs 15:1–2* —

Lord, my harsh words have gotten me into trouble more than I care to admit. I lack a filter to keep wrong things from coming out of my mouth which concerns me greatly. I do not mean to cause division and dissension but sometimes, I cannot help myself. I've always justified my opinion as me being blunt, honest, and forthcoming, but not everyone appreciates my direct approach. At times, what I say can come across as cold, and the message I intended to convey gets lost in translation. I am not one who could care less what others might think, but I feel like I am hopelessly alone on an island. I want to create peace with my words but all I tend to do is stir the pot with others. Why am I so divisive? Do I not possess self-control to tame my tongue?

The enemy would have me believe I've done nothing wrong stating my opinion because I am just being true to myself. I am tempted to believe it is not my problem if others are offended by what I say. Why then should I change to appease someone's feelings? That attitude only fuels my pride and points to everyone else being the problem, not me. How can I continue to be so blind? My response is my responsibility. No matter what the enemy would have me believe, I know that I have the power to bless others or curse them with my words. Thus, help me recognize the error of my ways so I can guard my tongue more wisely. I want to be slow to speak and quick to listen, but I cannot turn from wickedness if I am devoid of Your truth in my life. Instead, I need a clean heart and proper discernment to filter my words daily. Amen.

Who Cares?
(Drudgery)

*"I hated all my toil in which I toil under the sun, seeing that I must leave
it to the man who will come after me, and who knows whether he will be
wise or a fool? Yet he will be master of all for which I toiled and
used my wisdom under the sun. This also is vanity."*

— Ecclesiastes 2:18–19 —

Lord, I just don't care anymore. I am sick and tired of feeling burnt out. Mentally, the tread on my tires is completely worn down, and I have lost my grip on what is profoundly important. For years, I felt like a hamster on a wheel, running in circles with no end in sight. I lament the amount of time I wasted chasing after pleasures of this world to keep up with the status quo. I have accumulated wealth throughout my life but for what purpose? None of it goes with me when I die, so why have I exhausted myself only to leave it all behind? Time could have been better spent investing in relationships and giving generously to others rather than storing up pleasures for myself.

Satan has a way of making me second guess decisions I have made. He wants me to wallow in guilt, shame, and regret for time I've wasted accumulating money, power, and fame. In many ways, I wish I could go back and change my past. Nevertheless, who I am today is not a product of folly and misfortunate because it led me to this moment of self-reflection. I now see that life is not about vast accumulation but generosity. Help me use all You have given to bless others. Let my fists not be tightly clenched but open to opportunities You provide to be a minister of Your grace. Please forgive me for not recognizing it before, Lord. I commit to sharing all You have blessed me with so You may be glorified. Thank You for Your sovereign provision which humbles me daily. I am eternally grateful. Amen.

Naked and Afraid
(Vulnerability)

*"Therefore, confess your sins to one another and pray for one another,
that you may be healed. The prayer of a righteous person
has great power as it is working."*

— James 5:16 —

Lord, I have never enjoyed bearing my soul to others. Confessing sin makes me feel extremely uncomfortable, but I know You want me to embrace vulnerability, not hide from it. All of my life, I have kept others at arm's length, not letting anyone draw too close and know my dirty secrets. In many ways, pride has held me back from being completely honest. Fear is my primary concern because of what others might think of me. In either case, You call me to expose the darkness of my heart and share my life with others. For when I do, Your name is glorified because You draw me out of darkness and into the light of grace and mercy where healing is found.

When I confess my sins, Satan is also stripped of his power to hold me captive and torment my mind. That is why he sinks his teeth deeper into my flesh to hold me back from sharing my story. Truly, I am not accustomed to being emotionally naked before others. If people knew what I struggle with, they might never look at me the same. I may be shunned, persecuted, criticized, or condemned. Only You know what reaction I will receive for facing my fears and being vulnerable with others but give me strength and courage to trust Your Spirit's leading. The enemy will not stop trying to make me afraid of the unknown, but I know You are with me no matter how dark the road may be. Give me fortitude to trust Your will and confidence to know my life is not devoid of purpose but divinely inspired by Your Spirit to glorify the precious name of Jesus. Amen.

Dripping with Arrogance
(Arrogance)

"Talk no more so very proudly, let not arrogance come from your mouth; for the LORD is a God of knowledge, and by him actions are weighed."

— *1 Samuel 2:3* —

Lord, please forgive me for being so arrogant to sin against You yet act as if I can stand righteous before Your throne. My mind is depraved and my heart consumed with lusts of the flesh. I have been so focused on satisfying my own desires that I disregarded Your Word and sinned against You. Why am I prone to wander? Why is it difficult to use self-control and reject temptation? Your Word teaches me to not think more highly of myself than I ought (Rom. 12:3), but I fail miserably with laying down my pride at the foot of Your cross. It is humbling to admit how arrogant I have become. I assume I can control my appetite for guilty pleasures, but reality paints a different picture of weakness I am unwilling to accept. I want to believe I have enough self-control to say, "No!" to temptation, but I am sorely mistaken.

I don't want to be prideful. That is not my intention at all. Still, it is easy to minimize or justify my sins as a necessary evil to avoid falling victim to something greater. How sick have I truly become? Why is the power of darkness so prevalent in my life? Help me approach Your throne of grace with a humble and penitent attitude. I do not want to be like the Pharisee who boasted of his good deeds at the expense of his neighbor (Luke 18:9-14). Rather, compel me to cry out, "Lord, be merciful to me, a sinner!" My life has no meaning if You are not at the center of everything I say and do. Please forgive me for being naïve and arrogant to think I am anything apart from Your grace. I do not want to drip with arrogance but thankfulness for all You have done in my life. Let me boast in You, Lord, for You alone are worthy. Amen.

Misery Loves Company

(Misery)

"Now when Job's three friends heard of all this evil that had come upon him, they came each from his own place... And when they saw him from a distance, they did not recognize him. And they raised their voices and wept and tore their robes and sprinkled dust on their heads toward heaven."

— Job 2:11–12 —

Lord, my heart is in mourning. I lament days gone by when life was easier to manage and more enjoyable. Now, I am faced with trials. Calamity has come upon me. Pain and suffering are commonplace. I see no end in sight to deliver me from despair. All I have are regrets for what could have been had life not take a drastic turn toward misery. I am thankful, though, for those who have met me in the valley and offered condolences for my sorrow. Please pardon me for isolating myself rather than receiving their words of encouragement. As strange as it sounds, I am perfectly content wallowing in despair. I know my poor attitude is a dangerous weapon capable of impacting those who wish to help me. I just pray that my misery does not impact them.

Why am I so depressed? Is my pain and sorrow so great that You cannot overcome them? I fear my faith is too weak to trust the plans You have for me. I have struggled to find silver-linings of Your grace amid my troubles and taken my frustrations out on loved ones. Please forgive me for not appreciating the wise counsel You provide. Those who are willing to sit in the valley with me deserve better. I do not wish to be a burden to others, but I know that I need help. Thank You for sending messengers of healing and peace to my weary soul. I do not deserve the love which has been poured out on me, but I receive it with gladness and thanksgiving. I praise You for loving me when I am least unlovable. Amen.

Caution to the Wind

(Recklessness)

"The simple believes everything, but the prudent gives thought to his steps.
One who is wise is cautious and turns away from evil,
but a fool is reckless and careless."

— *Proverbs 14:15–16* —

Lord, I have taken many risks in life. Some big. Some small. I also have scars to prove Your Word is true because life has taught me that being careful is wise. When I was young, I threw all caution to the wind. I felt invincible—able to conquer the world by the sweat of my brow. Time has humbled me, though, and shown me that a fool is reckless because he thinks only of himself. There are many who count on me to be there when called upon. My life does not exist in a vacuum where decisions I make have no bearing on others. Quite the contrary! I am loved which forces me to reevaluate whether my careless behavior is worth it. What residual impact could my misfortune have if I took a risk which produced grave consequences? It is sobering to consider how little thought I have given to my constant risk-taking.

The enemy is quick to capitalize on my wishful curiosity. The thrill of the hunt for newfound pleasure can be intoxicating. It could also cost me my life if I am not careful. Why am I so prone to adventure? Aren't risks a part of life, for better or worse? What I need is wisdom and discernment to determine if the risks I take are worth it. At this point, I just don't know. What I do know is that reading Your Word is critical to survival. Moreover, I must pray without ceasing and allow the Holy Spirit to reveal what I need to know in the moment. Help me to not be dissuaded by fear but prudent to count the costs before throwing all caution to the wind. Your Word is life, and I am wise to follow its precepts every day of my life. Amen.

Checked Out
(Indifference)

"Behold, I stand at the door and knock. If anyone hears my voice and opens the door, I will come in to him and eat with him, and he with me."

— Revelation 3:20 —

Lord, how many times have You knocked upon my door but I did not answer? How many times have You called my name and I refused to acknowledge? My mind has become cold and calloused to the sound of Your voice. Weeds of indifference have choked the life out of what spiritual fruit I have left in my possession. I am struggling to find love, joy, peace, patience, kindness, goodness, faithfulness, gentleness, and self-control in my life. What I feel is numbness and apathy toward the world around me. I have lost any desire to fight for what I believe in. When I look around, I see a culture at war with itself and I want no part of it. I am tired and weary of senseless arguments. I want to unplug from reality, but I know that is not Your will for my life. You expect me to answer when You knock and obey Your Word despite how indifferent I feel.

Why has my heart become so hardened? At what point in my faith journey did I check out and stop caring? Indifference scares me more than I care to admit. I do not want to be insensitive to the needs of others nor miss an opportunity to bless them. I know that I cannot be a light in this world without Your eternal flame illuminating through me. Help me answer when You knock and trust the plans You have for my life. No matter how difficult the road may be, I will yield to Your sovereign will and guard my heart from thinking I know best. The enemy wants me to remain idle, but I cannot allow his voice to be the one I follow. Instead, help me wait in eager anticipation for the day You knock upon my door so that I do not miss it. Amen.

Pruning Season

(Sanctification)

*"I am the true vine, and my Father is the vinedresser.
Every branch in me that does not bear fruit he takes away, and every
branch that does bear fruit he prunes, that it may bear more fruit."*

— John 15:1–2 —

Lord, as seasons of my life pass by, I am reminded that pruning is a necessary evil which must come to fruition. I cannot expect to grow in my faith if I am not sold out for Christ and applying Your Word throughout my life. I am thankful for the work of the Holy Spirit living in me, but at times I fail to produce a harvest in return. Like a grape which has fallen from the vine, I do not always bring forth good fruit which is pleasurable to eat. Sometimes, I allow the fruit of the Spirit to rot away without realizing it. What I pray is that the lessons I have learned will allow seeds of righteousness to grow once more. I cannot experience all the plans You have for me if I resist seasons of pruning, so help me be obedient and give You full access to my heart.

I am too scared to ask how many branches You have pruned from my life over the years. Knowing the depravity of my heart, I can only begin to imagine! Nevertheless, the work You are doing within me is incredible. With intricate precision, You convict me of sin and force me to decide whether I'll allow You to perform surgery upon my heart. I am thankful You have honored my request to cleanse my mind and renew a steadfast spirit within me which is sold out to honor You. I cannot begin to imagine where my life would be if You had not pulled me out of the grave I was digging for myself. I need constant pruning in my life, so please have Your way with me. Give me fresh eyes to see the light of Your grace and a willingness to continually bow in reverence to Your holy presence. Amen.

Heart's Cry

(Restraint)

"Therefore I will not restrain my mouth; I will speak in the anguish of my spirit; I will complain in the bitterness of my soul."

— Job 7:11 —

Lord, for far too long, I have bottled up my emotions. Oftentimes, I do not know what to say or how to express what I am feeling. It is just easier to remain silent and wait till later to work through it all. The problem is I rarely go back and reconcile my thoughts. Before I know it, I am onto something else. Satan distracts me from expressing how I'm feeling. He does not want me to reconcile anything but keep everything bottled up. He knows that I will eventually explode when enough pressure is exerted against my mind. At that point, all bets are off at to what I will say and do, and that unpredictability has the potential to do great damage. Why am I so hesitant to express how I feel? I am doing myself no favors by keeping a lid on my feelings or acting as if I don't care. That is a lie. I do care, and it is eating me up inside.

I am comforted knowing Job committed no sin restraining his mouth. He spoke plainly with how he felt. All things considered, he had everything in the world to complain about but did not sin when Satan afflicted him with many tragedies. It was not until he reflected upon his calamity that he could not hold it in any longer. He needed to purge his negative thoughts and feelings to You in prayer. I often feel guilty sharing everything that is on my mind with You. It does not feel right to criticize or complain, but I know You empathize with my weakness and do not judge me for releasing pent up frustrations. Help me to continually share my heart so I am not enslaved to emotions. Allow me to freely express the cries of my soul to You, so I may find everlasting peace in Your endless grace and mercy. Amen.

Cast Down

(Disgrace)

*"You know my reproach, and my shame and my dishonor;
my foes are all known to you. Reproaches have broken my heart,
so that I am in despair. I looked for pity, but there was none,
and for comforters, but I found none."*

— Psalm 69:19–20 —

Lord, I have been insulted, disgraced, and left for dead. My enemies have plunged me into despair, trampling my name and reputation for their benefit and pleasure. Friends walked away when I needed them most, but You have never forsaken me. Despite what pain and depression tempt me to believe, I am not alone, for You are with me. It is never easy being attacked for who I am. My identity as a Christ-follower has placed a target on my back. I know it has, for persecution is intense right now. The closer I draw near to You, the more spiritual warfare ratchets up all around me. It is difficult not to drift away into a state of hopelessness. I feel so alone. My heart is broken, and I have no one to lift my spirits in this valley of despair.

Please prevent my heart from wandering. I do not want to lose sight of where true north lies. No matter how isolated I feel, I know You have a plan and purpose for my life. Reproaches laid against me have no power to steal my joy if I do not let them. Help me fix my eyes on You despite the wind and waves swirling around me. When I step out of the boat and walk towards You, do not let fear take ahold of my heart nor tempt my mind to relent. Rather, give me confidence to look my oppressors in the eye and not be shaken. You have given me the power to be more than a conqueror in the face of evil. Please help me remember that nothing can separate me from Your love. I may feel alone at times, but You are always with me. Amen.

Innocence Lost

(Impurity)

"I adjure you, O daughters of Jerusalem, by the gazelles or the does of the field, that you not stir up or awaken love until it pleases."

— *Song of Solomon 2:7* —

Lord, I wish I had taken heed of Your Word long ago. I did not hold firm boundaries as I should have, and now I bear the scars of my actions. It is easy to awaken love without realizing it. One minute I was keeping my mind and body pure. The next, I gave in to desires and threw it all away. I am comforted knowing You restore the years the locust has eaten (Joel 2:25), but I lament what I wasted by giving in to temptation rather than remaining pure. Whether it be physical or not, I allowed my mind to wander and my body followed. Curiosity took over, and now I am left with questions as to what happened and why I relented to sin? I should have known better than to give ear to the enemy's lies, but I didn't. Consequently, I have nothing but regret to keep me company as I mourn the loss of my innocence.

Thank You for not making me feel worse than I already do. Shame has a way of reminding me how unworthy I am of Your grace. I know that is a lie, but it is how I feel when I look into the rearview mirror of my life and lament poor decisions I made. I cannot change my past but I can learn from it, and I praise You for helping me understand that nothing can separate me from Your love. I pray You would use my testimony as an encouragement for others to hold fast to their convictions and celebrate purity. What I have been through in my life is not devoid of purpose. Quite the opposite! I empathize with those who struggle to resist temptation because I know how it feels to relent to sin and suffer the consequences. Even still, thank You for restoring the joy of my salvation in Christ, for I am eternally grateful. Amen.

Socially Awkward

(Awkwardness)

*"God gave us a spirit not of fear but of power, love, and self-control.
Therefore, do not be ashamed of the testimony about our Lord."*

— 2 Timothy 1:7–8 —

Lord, I am not sure why, but I feel out of place in this community You have placed me in. I struggle being myself and feeling comfortable in my own skin. I have nothing to feel uneasy about. Yet, when the time comes to share my faith, I clam up. In an instant, I feel socially awkward to the point where I want to run and hide. Satan has certainly caused me to doubt whether I am smart enough, confident enough, or humble enough to be Your child. He plants seeds of doubt in my mind and distracts my attention away from talking about You. He makes me deathly concerned about what others might think of me. I am tired of giving ear to his lies for they cut deep. I have always felt inadequate sharing my testimony, and the spiritual warfare I feel is not helping. I get even more nervous opening up about why I struggle.

I am thankful You have placed people in my life who speak truth in love. Their affirmation and encouragement are desperately needed to help me sift fact from fiction on the battlefield of my mind. I never fully understood how important community is to spiritual survival, but the body of Christ has been a rock in my life. I may not be totally comfortable witnessing to others just yet, but I have not thrown in the towel and given up. I want to be used for Your glory which will require me to get comfortable with being uncomfortable. Your Spirit resides in my heart and I have nothing to fear. No one can harm me because my identity is in You, the author and perfector of my faith. Help me to stand boldly for Your Word and share how You have changed my life. I feel awkward, but I am made confident by Your Spirit. Amen.

True Replica

(Influence)

*"Beloved, do not imitate evil but imitate good. Whoever does good
is from God; whoever does evil has not seen God."*

— 3 John 11 —

Lord, who am I and what do I believe? Who have I allowed to sway my opinion and influence my decisions? Why have I given them such power? I have wrestled with questions such as these all my life. I am easily led astray when my guard is down, but my resolve to stick to a straight and narrow path is emboldened when I remain close to You. Life is full of fork-in-the-road moments in time. Discerning whether I should turn to the right of left is where I struggle. I want to live a holy and righteous life, yet the pleasures of this world draw me like a moth to a flame. I am torn between flesh and spirit. For **"the spirit indeed is willing, but the flesh is weak" (Matthew 26:41).** How can I remain committed to my salvation in Christ and resist temptation? What needs to change for me to imitate good instead of evil?

Thank You for speaking plainly to my heart through the power of Your Word. I long to imitate You as a beloved child and walk in Your footsteps. I am equally as concerned about protecting my mind from yielding to the enemy's schemes as committing evil acts which do not glorify You. Help me discern right from wrong. Give me clarity in moments of confusion. Lead me to Your absolute truth so I do not lean on my own understanding. Grant me discernment to avoid being led by emotions which are ever-changing. If I am to model my life after anyone, let me be a devout imitator of Jesus, my Lord and Savior. The enemy would have me believe I am too weak to resist temptation, but I know I am more than a conqueror through Christ who strengthens me. Thank You for that priceless gift. Amen.

Handle with Care

(Caution)

"Do your best to present yourself to God as one approved, a worker who has no need to be ashamed, rightly handling the word of truth."

— 2 Timothy 2:15 —

Lord, You have bestowed upon me a precious gift. Thank You for the absolute truth of Scripture which illuminates my path towards righteousness. I would have no clue how to live a godly life without Your Spirit guiding me (not that I have reached perfection). I am just a sinner saved by grace and unworthy to be called Your precious child. Words cannot describe how appreciative I am that You reached down into the pit of hell to redeem my soul. You gave Your life for me when I least deserved it. In turn, the least I can do is to consider Your Word seriously and follow its precepts all the days of my life. There are times, though, when my flesh is weak. I am careful to obey Your Word but I am also dismissive of it at times. Please forgive my foolishness. I am nothing apart from Your saving grace.

Help me plant my heart and mind beside the healing waters of Your Word. You quench my thirst and give me newfound appreciation for what it means to be rooted by streams of mercy. Even still, I worry that I will not live up to expectation and be the model citizen of heaven You desire. I am weak in heart, mind, and soul despite my best efforts to live a righteous life. Satan's grip tightens the more I yield to Your truth and reject temptation. Release his grip from my life and give me strength and courage to wield the sword of Your Spirit. Let my shield of faith keep the enemy at bay as I proclaim the name of Jesus to a lost and broken world. I am not who I should be, but by Your grace I am free to serve You. Help me declare how great You are so that others know the true source of my strength which is found in You. Amen.

Narcissistic Tendencies
(Narcissism)

"In the last days there will come times of difficulty. For people will be lovers of self, lovers of money, proud, arrogant, abusive, disobedient to their parents, ungrateful, unholy, heartless, unappeasable, slanderous, without self-control, brutal, not loving good, treacherous, reckless, swollen with conceit, lovers of pleasure rather than lovers of God, having the appearance of godliness, but denying its power. Avoid such people."

— 2 Timothy 3:1–5 —

Lord, when I read passages such as 2 Timothy 3:1-5, I cannot help but wonder whether the sins Paul listed in his letter describe me. Am I that self-absorbed and entitled? Do I love myself so much that I am solely focused on my own happiness, no matter the cost? It is easy to read a passage like this and quickly skim over it. My mind wants to categorize it as a warning to "those people" who do not know the Lord. However, the more I reflect and peel back the layers of my heart, I am convicted that it describes aspects of my character which must be reconciled and overhauled.

Though I am a Christian, I am not immune to succumbing to evil and living to please myself. The sad truth is I am often blind to my own blindness and fail to recognize my narcissistic tendencies. I mourn any semblance of self-posturing I exude which elevates myself over anyone else. Purge me of this wickedness! I am unworthy to be called Your child if I am being blatantly selfish to my own desires. Satan's power over my flesh is stronger than I realize, and I need Your surgical hand to remove this cancer from my heart. Help me die to self and turn from my wicked ways. I do not want to lead others astray nor be a stumbling block to Your Gospel. Thus, let the light of Christ shine in and through me as I humble myself daily before Your throne. Amen.

Clouded Judgment

(Legalism)

"Woe to you, scribes and Pharisees, hypocrites!
For you tithe mint, dill, and cumin and have neglected
the weightier matters of the law: justice, mercy, and faithfulness.
These you ought to have done, without neglecting the others.
You blind guides, straining out a gnat and swallowing a camel!"

— Matthew 23:23–24 —

Lord, I been so distracted by pettiness that I lost sight of what is truly important in life. I have been more focused on doing the bare minimum to check off a legalistic box than seeking opportunities to humble myself and focus on Your Word. How have I drifted so far off course? Why am I living with clenched fists instead of open hands? I am not eager to give generously and serve others. My perspective is backwards! I can just hear the enemy laughing, drawing my attention away from what You desire to teach me. If only I could go back and change my ways—that would be a precious gift! Alas, I am consumed by regret for not only disobeying You but leading others astray.

I repent of my sins and offer You a humble sacrifice of thanksgiving for Your grace and mercy. Second chances are precious gifts, and I intend to make the most of shifting my attention toward justice, mercy, and faithfulness rather than doing the bare minimum. I want to do the right thing, live the right way, and honor You in my thoughts and deeds. Yet I cannot do this alone, for Your Spirit empowers me to live for righteousness. What I need are fresh eyes to not only see the lost and hurting but help meet the needs of others in Your name. I pray that my life would be a pleasing sacrifice of faithfulness to You, for You have done great things in my life and I am forever thankful. Use me as You see fit, Lord, without reservation. Amen.

Certain Apprehension

(Apprehension)

"For all who are led by the Spirit of God are sons of God. For you did not receive the spirit of slavery to fall back into fear, but you have received the Spirit of adoption as sons, by whom we cry, 'Abba! Father!'"

— Romans 8:14–15 —

Lord, why am I afraid that something bad is about to happen? Why am I so prone to fear, doubt, and worry that I forget my identity in Christ? Anxiety plays no part in the life of one who is born-again and saved by the blood of the lamb, yet I continually default to waiting for the worst-case scenario to occur. Prior to coming to faith in Christ, I was enslaved to sin. I had no hope that I could be worthy of Your love, so I chased after the pleasures of this world and expected them to fulfill me. Satan held me in bondage to guilt and shame for so long that I accepted my sentence of eternal separation from You. I did not believe I could be worthy of Your grace, yet You extended it to me and saved my life from utter ruin. Now I stand before You cleansed and forgiven—rehabilitated, restored, and redeemed by Christ.

Why then am I so fearful? What once enslaved me holds no power over my life anymore, yet I succumb to anxiety daily. Is my faith weak? Is my salvation secure? How can I call myself a Christian but allow the enemy to hold my heart captive by fear? Like a loving father, You hold me close and calm my heart amid the storms of life. When lightning crashes and thunder rolls, You remind me that I am safe in Your arms. No power of hell can break the bond of salvation I have in Jesus. Help me step into my faith with renewed strength and courage to face doubt and apprehension with confidence. I am who I am because of Your love, and I never want to forget that I have power to destroy strongholds in Your mighty name. Amen.

Unqualified for Service

(Self-Doubt)

"But Moses said to the LORD, 'Oh, my Lord, I am not eloquent, either in the past or since you have spoken to your servant, but I am slow of speech and of tongue.' Then the LORD said to him, 'Who has made man's mouth? Who makes him mute, or deaf, or seeing, or blind? Is it not I, the LORD? Now therefore go, and I will be with your mouth and teach you what you shall speak.'"

— Exodus 4:10–12 —

Lord, You call me to step out in faith and be a light in a dark world. I am not so sure You called the right person, though. I am not a spiritual giant by any means. I struggle reading my Bible daily and feel awkward praying publicly. I don't always say the right thing or do what I am supposed to as a Christian. I often yield to fleshly desires when I should resist temptation and succumb to fear, doubt, and worry. There are far better people You could have chosen to accomplish Your will. I am just a hypocrite, unworthy to be of use to Your kingdom. Even still, You utilize me despite my faults. No excuse I attempt to use seems to matter because You see far greater potential in me than I ever could.

Why am I so insecure when it comes to proclaiming Your Gospel? I do not believe my faith is strong enough to move mountains. The enemy has succeeded in reinforcing how little I know about Your Word and how sinful I am. I shy away from defending my faith, for I do not know what to say. I feel so inept, yet it does not seem to matter to You. In some strange way, my sinful past allows me to empathize with those who are struggling. It takes a sinner to know one, so perhaps I am qualified to proclaim Your glory. I may not know the Bible as well as I should, but I know my story of salvation. Therefore, use me as You see fit, whatever that looks like in Your way and time. Amen.

Stumbling Block
(Role Model)

"Let us not pass judgment on one another any longer but rather decide never to put a stumbling block or hindrance in the way of a brother."

— Romans 14:13 —

Lord, the impact my behavior has on others concerns me. I worry about being a good example and not leading others astray. I know that my actions can draw others to You or push them away from Christianity. It is easy to minimize the impact I have on others, but You placed me where I am for a reason. I cannot ignore my personal responsibility to be the hands and feet of Jesus to a lost and broken world. What I do matters. I may not like it, but that is reality. My actions do not exist in a bubble. Rather, they set the tone for my life and magnify whether I am living according to Your Word. Oftentimes, I believe I am positioned directly at the center of Your grace. Other times, I feel like I'm stranded on a desert island with nothing but regret to keep me company.

It is difficult to accept that I am a role model. There are certain expectations which come with being a follower of Jesus, but I'm doing more damage than good when I take my salvation for granted and live to please myself. It is not my intent to disobey Your Word. I want to live for You so others find hope and healing in Jesus. However, the enemy wants me to live with regret over every little thing I have said and done (which is not God-honoring) to keep me enslaved. Granted, there are instances where I am prone to hypocrisy. In those moments, please forgive me for defiling Your great name. Satan can be relentless in his attacks against my character, but I know You will use me for Your glory so I do not lead others astray or become a stumbling block to their faith journey. Amen.

Unfinished Business

(Distractions)

"I have fought the good fight, I have finished the race, I have kept the faith. Henceforth there is laid up for me the crown of righteousness, which the Lord, the righteous judge, will award to me on that day, and not only to me but also to all who have loved his appearing."

— 2 Timothy 4:7–8 —

Lord, why do I have no issue starting something but never finishing it? That reality reigns true in my life both physically and spiritually. I have so many great ideas but struggle bringing them to fruition. I get easily distracted with the busyness of life and forget where I started or leave projects half-finished. My plight speaks to my inability to focus on one specific thing and see the process through from beginning to end. Unfortunately, my faith has suffered the same fate. When I first accepted Jesus as Lord and Savior, I was on fire for the Gospel. There was no end to my enthusiasm for Your grace as I ministered to the needs of others. That spark quickly faded, though, and now I sit idle wondering where the time has gone.

I do not want to be a Christian by name alone but a lightning rod for evangelism. I want to finish strong because I know my time is short and tomorrow is not guaranteed. I just cannot seem to maintain eternal perspective and a sense of urgency every day of my life. I lament all the years I wasted running hard out of the gate only to quickly drop back due to exhaustion. I did not have an endurance mentality to begin with, and spiritual immaturity inevitably became my downfall. Never again, though! Instill in me a consuming fire which the enemy cannot extinguish. Help me prepare for trials ahead which will attempt to derail my momentum. I cannot finish this race alone, but I trust You because You are my source of strength despite fatigue. Amen.

Highs and Lows

(Emotions)

"Answer me quickly, O LORD! My spirit fails!
Hide not your face from me, lest I be like those who go down to the pit.
Let me hear in the morning of your steadfast love, for in you I trust.
Make me know the way I should go, for to you I lift up my soul."

— Psalm 143:7–8 —

Lord, You have done great things in my life, far more than I could ask for or imagine. At the same time, I have endured trials which could have capsized my faith had I chosen to distrust Your sovereign will for my life. In every season, You have been faithful despite me feeling as if I was riding a rollercoaster, spiritually-speaking. I have seen countless lives changed for Your glory, but in the same token, my heart is prone to hopelessness and depression. Why? How can I be privy to signs and wonders of Your majesty yet wonder where You are in my life? This journey of faith You have me on is wrought with dangerous cliffs and bottomless caverns, but I have also sat upon summit peaks in awe of Your countless miracles.

How can I experience such highs and lows at the same time? I feel as if I need to level off my peaks and valleys so that my emotions are not all over the board. Even still, both extremes keep me dependent upon You. You are with me wherever I go and I thank You for proving that peace, joy, and happiness are found in Your grace and mercy. Thoughts and feelings come and go in an instant which means resting in Your presence is critical to my survival. It does not matter whether I am in seasons of plenty or famine. You calm my heart and give me peace to quell my anxious mind. Revive my soul and create a renewed spirit within me. I praise You for I am fearfully and wonderfully made to worship You all the days of my life. Amen.

Perfectly Imperfect

(Imperfection)

"For we all stumble in many ways. And if anyone does not stumble in what he says, he is a perfect man, able also to bridle his whole body."

— *James 3:2* —

Lord, please help, for I am consumed by a need to be perfect. I take my faith seriously and want to live for righteousness each day of my life. The problem is that no matter how hard I try, I fail to live exactly like Jesus. Sometimes, I am led by emotion and yield to my flesh. Temptation abounds and my heart relents to Satan's schemes far too often. Why can I not control my thoughts and actions? Is it an issue of self-control? Is my faith weak? Why can I not achieve perfection? If I call myself a Christian, I should be able to bridle my tongue, control my body, and filter my thoughts through Your Word. How many times have I failed You, though? Thousands? Millions? Satan continues to bait me into legalism by making me assume I must be perfect at all times. However, that expectation is crushing my psyche.

I cannot bear the weight of perfection and not fall victim to despair the moment I yield to sin. Give me fresh eyes to see Your Word clearly. While I am called to live for righteousness, I am not expected to be perfect. Rather, imperfections are just another reminder of why I must be wholly dependent on You as my source of strength. Let Your Spirit guide me so I would live for truth and proclaim Your name to the nations. I am far from perfect but You love me still. Thank You for that immeasurable gift. Help me to put perfection in its rightful place within my heart—as a goal I seek every day of my life which is impossible to attain. Guard my mind from the enemy and help me accept my imperfections as a constant reminder that You alone are perfect, not me. Amen.

Weight of Knowledge

(Ignorance)

"So whoever knows the right thing to do and fails to do it,
for him it is sin."

— James 4:17 —

Lord, why is it so hard to do the right thing? Why am I scared? What leaves my heart frozen with indecision? Your Spirit has illuminated Scripture to me and I am without excuse. I cannot act as if You did not speak to my heart when clearly You did. Knowledge weighs heavily on my mind but I am unsure how to lay apprehension at Your feet, take up my cross, and follow You. It is easy to preach but hard to live! These are the moments which define my faith or lack thereof, yet I am hesitant to release my grip on the comforts of life and follow wherever You lead. In many ways, I lean upon ignorance as a viable defense to avoid doing as You say. Nevertheless, I am without excuse because I was born into Adam's sin, and the knowledge of good and evil are ingrained in my heart, mind, and soul.

Knowing and doing are two different things, though. I cannot allow the enemy to tempt me into believing I can compartmentalize my faith as independent of works. What I do in this life reflects my beliefs, so I cannot call myself a Christian and not do what Scripture teaches. I am liable and held accountable to follow Your commands. I have no right to wish others well yet avoid meeting their needs. I am merely doing the devil's bidding by turning a blind eye to love my neighbor as Jesus would. Help me to not be a Christian by name alone. Let my actions honor You as I step outside my comfort zone, die to self, and obey the promptings You place upon my heart. Use me for Your glory and give me courage to step forward in faith and trust where Your Spirit leads. Amen.

Addiction Cravings

(Withdrawal)

"Like a dog that returns to his vomit is a fool who repeats his folly.
Do you see a man who is wise in his own eyes?
There is more hope for a fool than for him."

— Proverbs 26:11–12 —

Lord, I am tired—tired of fighting temptation, being an addict, and accepting the consequences of my actions. Sometimes, I want to end it all and escape reality. The straight and narrow path seems too daunting. I have tried to stay on it but my mind often veers off course, pulling me into sin with relative ease. I am afraid of relapsing, but these withdrawals are intense. My mind and body feel out of control and I do not know where to turn for help. Your Word comes across as dry and empty when I read it. Prayer feels cold and distant when I cry out to You. Nothing seems to quench this insatiable desire to end my pain and suffering except past addictions. How then can I remain pure and not yield to temptation? My mind is willing, but my flesh is weak.

Though the hours pass by excruciatingly slow, I will praise You for providing reprieve and helping me survive another day. I complain far too much about what I think You are not doing, but You are working all things together for my good whether I realize it or not. Life can be difficult and push me to the brink of complete ruin, but I know Your plans for me are far greater than what the enemy promises. Momentary pleasures will do nothing but keep me enslaved. Sin is intoxicating and addiction is merely relenting to sin on a consistent basis. Nevertheless, I know that I am not alone in my struggle. Help me choose You over the pleasures of this world. Withdrawals or not, I will fix my eyes upon Jesus when I step out of the boat and walk by faith until I reach the safety and security of Your loving arms. Amen.

All Bottled Up

(Volatility)

"A fool gives full vent to his spirit, but a wise man quietly holds it back."

— Proverbs 29:11 —

Lord, I have a lot on my heart and mind these days. Granted, many thoughts and opinions are not worth sharing, but there are some which warrant consideration. Should I express them or use restraint? It all depends, I suppose. I do not believe giving full vent to everything I think and feel is wise but expressing nothing at all is also problematic. I must have balance, but where do I draw the line? It is certainly easier said than done holding back my opinion. Satan would love for me to vent my thoughts when they enter my mind. He knows that immediate expression does not allow me to filter what I say or how I say it. As such, he wants me to react so that I fail to consider how my message will be received. It is why I often stuff my emotions and remain bottled up, though I know it is unwise because I am bound to explode.

When I read a verse like Proverbs 29:11, it feels like restraint is the wisest choice. In many cases, it is the best solution, yet I know that I cannot keep the lid shut on my emotions indefinitely. At some point, they need to come out so I can reconcile them in a healthy manner. Where I struggle is determining whether I should vent to You or include those I love into the equation. Discernment is key. Help me be prudent to ensure I am not being closed off but willing to share my heart with others. It is difficult to be vulnerable and admit when I am struggling. I would rather carry my cross all alone than burden others with how I think and feel. Undoubtedly, that is what Satan wants me to do. However, I am determined to filter my thoughts through Your Word so I am not held captive by bottled-up emotions but set free to worship You. Amen.

Own Worst Enemy
(Self-Deprecation)

*"And when you fast, do not look gloomy like the hypocrites,
for they disfigure their faces that their fasting may be seen by others.
Truly, I say to you, they have received their reward."*

— Matthew 6:16 —

Lord, I have come to realize that I can be my own worst enemy at times. I self-deprecate so as not to come across as prideful, but I am doing myself no favors when I beat myself up. Self-deprecation can be a slippery slope. On the one hand, modesty is a goal I should seek daily. However, if I am going above and beyond to make my penitence known, my contrition is less believable. Sometimes, I put myself down without realizing it—pointing out what I assume I have done wrong before allowing others the opportunity to state their opinion. I liken it to cooking dinner and making excuses for the meal before anyone has tasted it. Why am I quick to assume the worst? Why is my self-esteem so low that I undermine my self-worth?

I long to live a holy and righteous life. I have no interest being proud or arrogant but modest and humble. How then can I ensure my intentions are pure and honoring to You? Please give me clarity. The enemy has more than enough resources at his disposal to make me feel guilty for sinning against You. I certainly do not need to make his job easier by doing his work for him. Instead, I must examine my heart to ensure I am not blind to my own sin. The scarlet letter of guilt, shame, and regret is real, but it does not compare to Your unending grace and mercy. You died for my sins so I could walk in freedom, not bondage. Therefore, help me avoid the temptation to self-deprecate and know that humility is an issue of the heart which You examine thoroughly. Amen.

Out of My Control
(Helplessness)

"He must increase, but I must decrease."

— John 3:30 —

Lord, I am quickly learning that some things are completely out of my control. For instance, I cannot make the blind to see nor the deaf to hear. I will never be able to stop natural disasters or chronic illnesses from devastating countless lives. I cannot stop the reality of death nor the eternal separation which awaits those who deny salvation in Christ. I am completely helpless to do anything apart from Your grace and mercy. What I can do is control my response to life's trials and point others to Your Word for hope and healing. I can walk alongside those trapped in the valley of despair and love them in real and tangible ways. I can pray for the needs of others and fast on their behalf. In reality, there are many things I can control but others which are not my cross to bear. As such, I need wisdom and discernment to know what You would have me do.

It is a helpless feeling seeing people in sorrow and anguish but not knowing how to assist them. I want to step into the gap and help them navigate trials, but I am not their personal savior. Only You have the power to save, and I must guard my heart from taking Your place when it is never mine to begin with. That is the epitome of John 3:30 in my life today—knowing my place in Your kingdom and magnifying You in all ways. Please help me serve others and not fret about what is out of my control. I lack Your understanding. Only You know how to work all things together for good, and I must completely trust You to keep my sanity when all hope seems lost. Thank You for being in full control of my life, Lord. I never understood how precious a gift that was (and is) until now. Amen.

Negative to a Fault

(Negativity)

"And the people spoke against God and against Moses, 'Why have you brought us up out of Egypt to die in the wilderness? For there is no food and no water, and we loathe this worthless food.'"

— *Numbers 21:5* —

Lord, why am I so negative all the time? I feel trapped in a glass-half-empty world where pessimism is rampant and complaining is commonplace. I am too comfortable pointing out things I see that are wrong rather than looking for the good in people. I never intended to be such a pessimist, but cynicism befits me. Instead of appreciating a blue sky, I focus on the one dark cloud far off in the distance. I wish it was exhausting to be so critical, but negativity comes naturally to me. It is not something I am proud of, either, because it deters others from wanting to be around me. Why do I struggle looking on the bright side of life? What has made me so jaded towards everything I see? How can I give others the benefit of the doubt and not pick apart their faults and imperfections?

Your Word reminds me that discontentment is cancer. I cannot ignore Your sovereign provision yet expect You to continually bless me. Help me learn lessons from days of old when Your people spurned the countless miracles You provided in their hour of need. No matter what Satan tempts me to believe, You are good regardless of whether I am in seasons of feast or famine. Contentment is all about appreciating Your provision and looking for the silver-lining of grace and mercy in every corner of my life. I cannot begin to overcome negativity if I am looking at life from a glass-half-empty perspective. Rather, give me fresh eyes solely focused on counting my blessings so I can give You praise regardless of where life might take me. Amen.

Be Prepared
(Preparation)

"Stay dressed for action and keep your lamps burning and be like men who are waiting for their master to come home from the wedding feast, so that they may open the door to him at once when he comes and knocks."

— *Luke 12:35–36* —

Lord, how prepared am I for Your return? Am I wide awake or fast asleep? Is my faith strong enough to endure the enemy's attacks? Are my spiritual disciplines solid enough to keep me from wandering off into isolation? There are many disciplines in my faith journey which concern me, but only You can determine my maturity. I just struggle discerning whether I know Scripture well enough to defend my faith. How well do I pray without ceasing? Do I share the Gospel with others or hide in fear of man? Am I seeking opportunities to humble myself and serve my community, or am I living to please myself? Despite my questions and insecurities, I praise You for warning me to always be on guard. For I do not know whether I am at a point in my life where I am truly well-prepared and dressed for action, and that scares me.

Preparation is about planning for what lies ahead, but I am unsure about where You are leading me. I would never step foot into the wilderness without possessing skills and abilities which are critical for survival, and that same truth applies spiritually. Will I be able to withstand temptation when my flesh is weak and my mind is weary? Am I making You the center of my life so everything I say and do is filtered through Your Word? I think so, but I am not convinced. Therefore, help me to place my trust in You rather than my limited knowledge and abilities. If I rely upon myself, I will surely die. However, if I lean upon You as my strength, I will be able to endure spiritual warfare and stand ready and waiting for the day of Your return. Amen.

Fleshly Desires
(Temptation)

*"Let us walk properly as in the daytime, not in orgies and drunkenness,
not in sexual immorality and sensuality, not in quarreling and jealousy.
But put on the Lord Jesus Christ, and make no provision
for the flesh, to gratify its desires."*

— Romans 13:13–14 —

Lord, I am beaten, worn out, and tired. The enemy is attacking me from all sides and every angle. I cannot escape the countless traps he has lying in wait to ensnare my heart and mind. I feel like a ship adrift at sea. I am isolated and at the mercy of the wind and waves. I have nothing firm to anchor my life upon. There is no land in sight, just a never-ending horizon of blue which ravages my mind. How can I recalibrate my bearings? You are my true north, but I have lost all sense of direction. My body aches from relentless heat and chronic malnourishment. I need living water which only You can provide. I fear my resolve will not last, but I can only survive for so long before my body gives out and I succumb to temptation.

The desires of my flesh seem insatiable at times. The more I drink from the well of sin, the more I crave to keep me satisfied. The only problem is that immorality will never quench my thirst, so why do I drink the same poison expecting not to die? Do I honestly believe I can build a tolerance to sin by partaking in it more? Paul wrote, **"Are we to continue in sin that grace may abound? By no means! How can we who died to sin still live in it?" (Romans 6:1)**. I often think about what it means to be a Christ-follower. Abstaining from false idols is paramount! Am I succeeding, though? Please guard my heart and mind from yielding to temptation. Give me self-control to resist the desires of my flesh so I honor You in mind, body, and soul. Amen.

Dark Clouds

(Depression)

"Now is my soul troubled. And what shall I say? 'Father, save me from this hour'? But for this purpose I have come to this hour."

— John 12:27 —

Lord, there is a dark cloud which surrounds me, bringing torrential rain upon my soul. It refuses to leave but simply hovers overhead, mocking me with its never-ending gloom. Why me? What did I do to deserve this honor? I am bombarded with spiritual warfare on a daily basis and struggle holding the line. My heart is forever bound to You, but I am growing tired and weary. My mind has not seen the light of day in a while, and I fear it may never come again. Why is Satan so good at tempting me to despair? Why do I allow his voice to have any prevalence in my life? It makes no sense to fight the good fight and defend my position if I let down my guard. I refuse to waive the white flag of surrender, but my strength is fading. I have lost any desire to step outside when all I see is persistent rain.

Nevertheless, I will praise You despite my weakness. You make me strong by the power of Your Word. Help me remember how You led me to this point in my life. I go no place by accident and these trials are a steppingstone in my journey of faith. Thank You for empathizing with my troubled soul. You walked this lonely road long before I did and endured far more anguish than I could ever fathom. Even still, You did not abandon Your calling but stepped boldly into the fire and faced the enemy head-on. Give me courage to do likewise. These dark clouds may never leave me, but I will remain steadfast in my commitment to Your Word. You remind me that I am more than a conqueror through Christ who strengthens me, and I am thankful for Your gift of protection. Amen.

Insatiable Cravings
(Selfish Pleasure)

*"Therefore, since we are surrounded by so great a cloud of witnesses,
let us also lay aside every weight, and sin which clings so closely,
and let us run with endurance the race that is set before us."*

— Hebrews 12:1 —

Lord, the pleasures of this world can be intoxicating. The sweet aroma of sin is attractive to my senses but reveals its persistent stench when I yield to my flesh. It is so hard to remain pure of heart and mind. I long to escape the stress and anxiety in my life and not deal with burdens in my possession. Easier said than done, though. How can I find freedom from sin and not lean upon guilty pleasures to make it another day? Nothing in this world can satisfy my flesh, for it only craves more as time goes by. I know it mentally, but I am physically struggling to stay on a straight and narrow path toward You. I am worn out, run down, and on the brink of a breakdown if I do not find a solution to these insatiable cravings.

You know the intensity of my battle. You became flesh and thrust Yourself into the center of this world, enduring all that the gates of hell could throw at You. You were completely depleted and malnourished when the devil tempted You after forty days in the wilderness. Not once did You relent but held firm to Scripture as Your source of strength. Please help me to do likewise. Plant Your Word deep into the corners of my heart so I may never forget it. Fleshly cravings will only subside when I choose to no longer feed them but instead, replace them with healthy options. Instill a relentless desire within me to pray without ceasing and feast upon Scripture daily. Help me to long for righteousness as much as the false idols which have ensnared my heart and mind for far too long. Amen.

Reckless Abandon

(Recklessness)

"The simple believes everything, but the prudent gives thought to his steps.
One who is wise is cautious and turns away from evil,
but a fool is reckless and careless."

— *Proverbs 14:15–16* —

Lord, why do I feel out of control these days? My ability to corral my thoughts and filter my emotions has taken a substantial turn for the worst. I feel reckless, wild, and unrestrained—not living with wisdom and discernment but yielding to impulse at every turn. What is wrong with my heart? Why am I not giving more thought to what lies ahead and the consequences of my actions? The enemy often persuades me to lean on my own understanding instead of Your absolute truth. It is easier to live by instinct, but that is a slippery slope when I replace truth and wisdom with wishful thinking. I need boundaries and discipline to protect me from yielding to sin and also discernment to know the difference between right and wrong.

I have never been one who plays it safe all the time. I enjoy taking risks and seeing what happens. Granted, it is not a universal belief nor applicable in every situation. I do assess the risk of going too far and creating a wake of destruction in my path. I am not naïve to how dangerous fire can be. You have pulled me out of danger on countless occasions. I cannot thank You enough for saving me, but I pray You would help me avoid reckless desire. Free me from the thrill of taking risks which could damage my relationship with You. I am not invisible by any means but flawed in every way apart from Your grace. I do not deserve Your love, but I humbly praise You for drawing my heart to You in repentance. If I am to be reckless, let me live with a relentless pursuit of righteousness to know You more and do Your will. Amen.

Family Feud

(Family Tension)

*"But he answered his father, 'Look, these many years I have served you,
and I never disobeyed your command, yet you never gave me a young goat,
that I might celebrate with my friends. But when this son of yours came,
who has devoured your property with prostitutes, you killed the fattened
calf for him!' And he said to him, 'Son, you are always with me, and all
that is mine is yours. It was fitting to celebrate and be glad, for this
your brother was dead, and is alive; he was lost and is found.'"*

— Luke 15:29–32 —

Lord, I am tired of friction at home. Whether it be my immediate or extended family, I despise conflict with loved ones. There is a chasm that exists between those who follow You and those who reject the truth of Your Word. For me, I cannot turn a blind eye toward sin nor appease family members who blatantly disregard Your moral law. I pray their eyes be opened, but I refuse to ease their conscience by minimizing or justifying sin. I mourn for them because I relate to their plight. I once rebelled against You and sought to satisfy the desires of my flesh. I was bound to eternity in hell if not for Your salvation.

I also know what it means to be eternally washed clean, and I pray for my loves ones who have wandered off into the wilderness. What they seek to fulfill them is a mirage. I know it well. I once drank sand thinking it would quench my thirst, but I do not want others to make the same poor choices. Please bind the enemy from driving a root of bitterness within my family relationships. Help me endure persecution knowing that those who attack me are rejecting You, not me. Keep my heart from yielding to sin and guard my tongue so the words I speak point them to Your grace and mercy. Let us not be estranged but instead, come together one day united in spirit and truth. Amen.

Split Personality
(Personal Identity)

"For I do not understand my own actions.
For I do not do what I want, but I do the very thing I hate."

— Romans 7:15 —

Lord, it seems as if my attitude and temperament can change on a dime. One minute, I'm calm. The next minute, I'm stressed. Why can I not seem to get a handle on my emotions? I can go from happy to sad or peaceful to discontent so quickly. How then do I manage my feelings and take every thought captive to obey Christ (2 Cor. 10:5)? I struggle understanding how my flesh has such power over my faith and trust in You. I know Your Word. I believe it wholeheartedly. Still, something within me shifts when temptation rises to the forefront of my mind. It is as if I am willing to trade my eternal birthright for a bowl of soup like Esau did. I lose my sense of the big picture and focus on momentary pleasures which are fleeting. I also yield to temptation and not fight against it. Why? Is my faith truly that weak? How can I call myself a Christian and not apply what the Bible teaches?

I praise You for being patient with me despite my failures. I do not want to have chameleon-like faith where I blend into culture around me. I want to hold fast and stand firm on the foundation of Your Word, come what may. Help me be more consistent in my life so others see You in a positive light. I never want my actions to contradict Scripture, but I have done more damage than good over the years with my "Dr Jekyll and Mr. Hyde" personality. Please forgive me. Help me ensure I am the same person publicly as privately. You pulled me out of the darkness and I praise You for giving me new life that I may proclaim Your glory. Unify my heart and mind so my actions and Your Word do not contradict each other but are one in the same. Amen.

Unspoken Words
(Missed Opportunities)

"And we urge you, brothers, admonish the idle, encourage the fainthearted, help the weak, be patient with them all. See that no one repays anyone evil for evil but always seek to do good to one another and to everyone."

— *1 Thessalonians 5:14–15* —

Lord, I regret the number of missed opportunities You have given me to bless others. Whether family, friends, or total strangers, I've neglected to be Your hands and feet of grace and mercy. I dare say my immediate family does not know how I feel about them. My friends suffer from the same fate. I fail to see the power of my words because they seem insignificant. I assume those around me know how I feel about them, so what need is there to formally express my opinion? Few people have taken time to encourage me throughout my life. Why then is it important to exhort and admonish others? What difference does it make whether I express my heart or keep feelings to myself?

With every excuse I use to deflect my responsibility to obey Your Word, I am reminded that tomorrow is not guaranteed. When I look upon my past, there are conversations I missed because I thought I had more time. Truly, seasons change and death is inevitable. Time has robbed me from being a blessing to others due to insecurity and pride. I have been too scared to express my heart to others, and words have been left unspoken for far too long. However, not all time is lost. I can still make the most of today and speak truth in love to those around me. I simply need to be open to Your Spirit and willing to obey when He calls me to speak on Your behalf. You are gracious and loving, Lord, and I wish to be that kind of light in the lives of those I know and those You will direct my path toward in the future. Help me share the Gospel at all times that others may be greatly encouraged. Amen.

Gone with the Wind

(Mortality)

"He will wipe away every tear from their eyes, and death shall be no more,
neither shall there be mourning, nor crying, nor pain anymore,
for the former things have passed away."

— *Revelation 21:4* —

Lord, death is the great equalizer in life. At some point, we will all experience it. When I look back upon my story, many faces come to mind—lives which have tremendously impacted who I am today, for better or worse. Some have blessed me. Others hurt me. Granted, I must live with the memories of both, but I can mourn them as well. Not everyone's life has a happy ending. I have seen loved ones die unexpectedly while others experienced slow deterioration. One could argue that sudden death is better than prolonged agony. Still, it does not matter. They are no longer with me and I lament their passing. A portion of my heart feels missing, yet I do not know how to remedy the pain. I know You can fill my cup until it overflows, but I struggle reconciling why my loved ones are no longer here. I will never fully understand Your plans, but I trust You will always comfort my soul.

Where I take great solace is knowing that my loved ones who were born-again and saved by grace through faith in Christ. They are waiting for me in heaven—free of pain, worry, and sorrow. They have seen the joy of their salvation completed, and it soothes my aching heart knowing they are in a better place. In the same token, I mourn those who have rejected Your salvation. I will never see them again which makes me look at death very differently. It is a reminder that I am just a vapor—here today and gone tomorrow. Therefore, give me eternal perspective to make the most of the time You have given me to share Your Gospel and point others towards salvation in Christ. Amen.

Nervous Breakdown

(Nervousness)

"The LORD is my shepherd; I shall not want. He makes me lie down in green pastures. He leads me beside still waters. He restores my soul. He leads me in paths of righteousness for his name's sake."

— Psalm 23:1–3 —

Lord, I feel like I am on the verge of a nervous breakdown. Almost everything bothers me these days. I am irritated, frustrated, and angry. No one can relate to how I am thinking and feeling because they do not shoulder my particular burdens on a daily basis. If I fail to do something, it will not get done (or at least done properly). The only one I can rely on is myself, and that is what Satan wants me to believe. My life feels like a constant headache which never subsides. Pressure continues to mount against me from all sides and every angle, yet I am determined to grind my way through life no matter the cost. What I am learning is that carrying my burdens alone is crushing my psyche. It embitters me towards the ones I love and plunges me into despair.

Why can I not seem to release my grip on every detail of my life? I want to trade my sorrows and live in the light of Your grace, but I do not know how. I am nowhere near a peaceful state of mind but I need Your immediate help or else I will fall into depression. Only You have the power to save me, for You lead me besides still waters. The only reason I am alive today is because You loved me enough to die in my place. Help me to not be distracted by every detail of life which seems out of place. Rather, teach me to rejoice in life's imperfections. Give me perspective to not sweat the small stuff but instead, cast my cares at the foot of Your cross. The only way I can overcome these thoughts and emotions is to give You full control of my life. As such, have Your way in my heart and grant me everlasting peace. Amen.

Impulse Reaction

(Impulsiveness)

*"Know this, my beloved brothers: let every person be quick to hear,
slow to speak, slow to anger; for the anger of man does not
produce the righteousness of God."*

— James 1:19–20 —

Lord, if there is one nugget of wisdom I have learned the hard way, it would be that my response is my responsibility. How often do You and I rehash this one principle together? It seems like an everyday occurrence because I fail to learn my lesson. Whatever enters my mind exits through my mouth almost simultaneously without the slightest regard for how it may be received. I have gotten myself in trouble far too often for not placing a filter on my tongue. What You have taught me, though, is that wisdom comes from being quick to listen and slow to express my thoughts. The reality is not everyone wants to hear what I have to say. They have grown accustomed to my sharp words and would rather tune me out than consider my opinion. It is sad to say, but I have worn out my welcome with many people.

I am thankful that You never stop me from expressing my raw and honest feelings with You. However, I cannot expect those around me to respond similarly with long-suffering love and patience. Their rope is much shorter and I fear that if I do not get a handle on my impulse reactions, I will burn more bridges than mend them. Give me discernment to know when to speak vs. when to hear. Help me to esteem the opinions of others as equal to my own. You speak truth to me in many ways and sometimes, it comes in the most unexpected ways. I pray that I am no longer blind to my own blindness but eager to know how I can change for the better. I am not perfect by any means but help me to be perfected by Your truth so my words glorify Jesus. Amen.

For Better or Worse

(Ownership)

"I will restore to you the years that the swarming locust has eaten,
the hopper, the destroyer, and the cutter, my great army,
which I sent among you."

— Joel 2:25 —

Lord, for better or worse, I am who I am. My life is filled with land mines which have detonated relationships, maimed those I love, and left me incapacitated with guilt, shame, and regret. The worst part is that I have no one to blame but myself. I was arrogant and selfish, and now I am reaping what I sowed due to naïve foolishness. Had I sought Your Word for wisdom, I would likely not be looking into the rearview mirror with lament. As it stands, I am overwhelmed with grief. How could I have trampled underfoot the hearts of those who loved me at my worst. How could I take their forgiveness for granted and revel in worldly pleasures at their expense? Who could do such a thing and not suffer the consequences?

Though I do not deserve a second chance, I praise You for loving me despite my evil ways. Your blood has washed away my sin. I have no other response but humble reverence before Your judgment seat. Not only do You redeem me, but You allow me to enter Your presence in prayer and meditation. The enemy has no hold on me because the victory is Yours. Thank You, Jesus! I may not be the righteous child You call me to be, but I am not who I once was and that is a miracle. Help me to use my story as a testimony of Your grace and mercy to lost souls. If anything, my life is a redemptive miracle of restoration, and You are the author of heart change. Please bind the enemy's grip on my mind and give me fresh eyes to see Your glory each day. You gave me a new story which glorifies You, and I am ever grateful. Amen.

Leaving an Inheritance

(Legacy)

"Whatever you do, work heartily, as for the Lord and not for men, knowing that from the Lord you will receive the inheritance as your reward. You are serving the Lord Christ."

— *Colossians 3:23–24* —

Lord, when I reach the end of my life, what will my legacy be? Will I be remembered positively or negatively? I cannot begin to count the number of poor choices I have made throughout my life. Satan made quite the mess of me until I came to faith in Jesus. The only difference between now and then is the power of the cross which saved a wretch like me. The older I get, the more I wonder if I made the most of the time You allotted. In some ways, I believe so. In others, I mourn the time I wasted chasing worldly pleasures to the detriment of my relationship with You. Who I am and who I was are forever intertwined. They provide context to why I cried out to You for salvation. I am so thankful that You heard my distress, though, because my life has been transformed for Your majesty.

Nevertheless, the enemy whispers lies into my ears and tempts me to view my life as a colossal failure. He wants me to wallow in the reality of my imperfections—that I will never be good enough to enter the kingdom of heaven one day. The sad truth is he is right. I will never be good enough to stand justified before You on judgment day, but I am given free passage because Jesus paid my debt. If there is one legacy I wish to leave others, it would be my story of redemption. I once was blind, but now I see. That is the only story worth remembering because it magnifies the immeasurable sacrifice You made on the cross for me. Therefore, I will spend my days pointing others to Christ. My legacy is Yours and that is what truly matters when I breathe my last. Amen.

Light in the Darkness

This was an incredibly difficult book to write. Many friends and loved ones prayed for me as I fought my way through it. I cannot begin to convey how much Satan opposed me on this project. I write prayers all the time for chapters in my books, but this was a completely different project to compose. At times, it felt like it would never reach completion. Reason being, I had to immerse myself in dark and heavy emotions to experience the stress and anxiety of each topic. It weighed upon my psyche and tempted me to abandon what the Lord called me to write. What ensued, though, was the epitome of what lamentations is all about—laying my raw and vulnerable emotions at the feet of Jesus and refreshing my soul with the absolute truth of His Word.

I empathize with those struggling to reconcile the darkness of their thoughts and feelings. Reflective prayer is not for the faint of heart. It seems like it should be easy to cry out to God, but it can be extremely difficult. I was forced to examine the darkest corners of my soul and reconcile things I had locked up and thrown away the key. Satan's countless lies were exposed as I immersed my mind into each raw emotion. Guilt, shame, and regret were constant companions along this faith journey, but so was the Holy Spirit who never allowed the enemy to condemn me. Rather, conviction overwhelmed my soul and drew me closer to Jesus as His glory was magnified in my weakness.

Truly, this prayer anthology was a grind. I fought the potential of redundancy—each page sounding the same. In ways, the structure of each prayer is identical: honest confession and fervent self-preaching. Yet, what adds color to the page is the uniqueness of each topic and how the Lord spoke to me when I allowed my mind to dive deep into the valley of despair. I discovered that my thoughts and feelings are far more complex than I realized. The same root exists but each branch is unique. I also learned that God can withstand the onslaught of my raw and unfiltered emotions. He is not put off by my countless questions either. Instead, He listened closely to the meditations of my soul and answered each one through the power of His Word.

I never realized how much I needed the Lord to shine light into the darkness of my heart until I began this project. It allowed me to purge thoughts and emotions I had bottled up for too long. It also enabled me to reconcile bitterness and confusion, but I had to journey deep into the wilderness of my mind to find lasting peace. Like Jesus, I was tempted to throw in the towel and give up. I was tired and weary. My body was worn down, and I struggled to find meaning in it when the enemy attacked me at every turn. However, the absolute truth of the Gospel became my saving grace. I was able to not only defend myself but inflict lethal blows to demons which haunted my mind.

The lovingkindness of Jesus Christ became real to me as I journeyed through each prayer. He reminded me that I was not alone, and His assurance enabled me to pick myself up from the ashes and stand in the light of His grace, love, and mercy. I cannot begin to describe how freeing it is to release mental and emotional burdens once and for all. The joy of my salvation became the cornerstone of victory over sin and darkness in my life. As a result, I cannot help but praise my Lord and Savior, for He loved me despite my faults and insecurities and saved me when I was floundering in shame and regret.

The power of the Gospel is that it draws sinners to repentance. I found hope and healing each time Satan attacked my heart and mind. When I opened my Bible and began reading, I discovered how I am more than a conqueror through Christ who strengthens me. Thus, it is imperative that I abide in Him at all times. The moment I drift away from His presence, darkness begins to fill my mind. Therefore, I must cling to His Word daily, for His mercies are new every morning and I need them desperately to survive the troubles of this fallen world.

Attributes of a Godly Marriage

Is your marriage healthy, struggling, or somewhere in between? Are you enjoying marriage to the fullest or battling with frustration and discontentment? **"Attributes of a Godly Marriage"** is a 52-day devotional designed to help engaged, newlywed, and married couples know what it means to love one another like Jesus would. It provides wisdom and clarity around the keys to a God-honoring marriage by filtering our wedding vows through a Biblical lens. Moreover, it helps identify the root cause of most marital issues and provides practical advice on how to remedy the problem. Most of all, it encourages couples to appreciate the true blessing of marriage by shifting our attention from what we think we need to be happy and refocusing our efforts on how to love our spouse sacrificially "till death do us part."

Target Audience: Men and Women (Couples or Singles)

Distant From God

Do you struggle with prayer? Many do. Praying is a common weakness in the church today. We assume everyone knows how to pray, but nothing could be further from the truth. Sadly, many of us walk away from prayer rather than drawing near to the Lord. We are unable to experience its full power because our insecurities, anxieties, and self-doubt hold us back.

"Distant From God: Why the Struggle to Pray is Real" is a 40-day devotional designed to address the importance of prayer, why we struggle to pray, and how we can build a deeper relationship with Jesus. Whether you are someone who doubts the power of prayer, or someone who is looking to deepen your spiritual life, this book will challenge and encourage you to lift your heart to God and grow in your understanding of prayer.

Target Audience: Men, Women, and Teens.

Lord, I'm Tired

Have you ever asked yourself the following questions: Why am I so overwhelmed by fear, doubt, and worry? How can I resist giving up when the storms of life tempt me to lose faith? What is God's plan and purpose for my life when it feels like the walls are closing in around me? Why do I feel so tired and helpless, crushed by the weight of pain and confusion?

"Lord, I'm Tired," unpacks twenty issues which consume our minds, directing our attention toward God's Word for answers to life's trials. Whether enslaved to sin or struggling to resist temptation, we can discover hope and healing in the absolute truth of holy Scripture which casts light into the darkness of our hearts. All we need is to focus our attention on Jesus Christ to find rest for our weary souls and discover the peace of God which surpasses all understanding (Phil. 4:7).

Target Audience: Men, Women, and Teens.

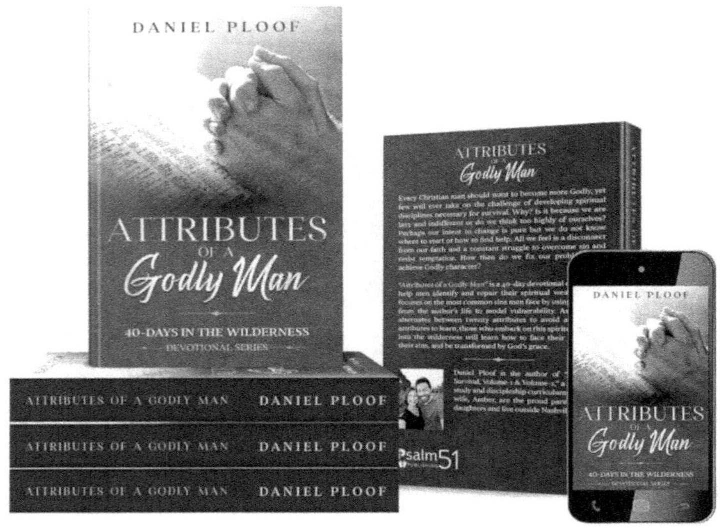

Attributes of a Godly Man

Every Christian man should want to become more Godly, yet few will ever take on the challenge of developing spiritual disciplines necessary for survival. Why? Is it because we are lazy and indifferent or do we think too highly of ourselves? Perhaps our intent to change is pure but we do not know where to start or how to find help. All we feel is a disconnect from our faith and a constant struggle to overcome sin and resist temptation. How then do we fix our problems and achieve Godly character?

"Attributes of a Godly Man" is a 40-day devotional designed to help men identify and repair their spiritual weaknesses. It focuses on the most common sins men face daily by using examples from the author's life to model vulnerability. As each day alternates between twenty attributes to avoid and twenty attributes to learn, those who embark on this spiritual journey into the wilderness will learn how to face their fears, own their sins, and be transformed by God's grace.

Target Audience: Men, Women, and Teens.

Wilderness Survival

Men's Bible Study/Discipleship Curriculum

Embark on a journey of survival training deep in the spiritual wilderness of isolation where few men dare to venture. Explore forty personal issues every man deals with in his life and marriage. Embrace the ultimate accountability challenge to become the man, husband, and father God calls you to be by transforming your life and changing your behavior.

"Wilderness Survival" is all about building Godly spiritual disciplines and surrendering to God's authority by examining your heart and filtering it through the absolute truth of His Word. The more you learn to guard your mind, the greater chance you will have of surviving the wilderness seasons of life and marriage, restoring the joy of your salvation, and defeating the enemy once and for all.

Target Audience: Men in relationships; preparatory for singles.

About The Author

Daniel Ploof is the author of several Christian-living books, Bible studies, and devotionals including: **"Attributes of a Godly Marriage: From: 'I Do' To: 'I Will!'" "Distant From God: Why the Struggle to Pray is Real," "Lord, I'm Tired: Gospel Truth for a Restless and Weary Soul," "Attributes of a Godly Man,"** and **"Wilderness Survival, Vol-1 & Vol-2."**

He is also the founder of **"Wilderness Survival Training,"** a resource platform designed to help Christian men and women find wisdom and discernment in God's Word. For more information and access to reflections, devotionals, and discipleship resources, please visit: **https://www.journeyintothewilderness.com.**

Daniel has been married to the love of his life and best friend, Amber, for over twenty-four years. They are the proud parents of four amazing daughters who are their greatest treasures this side of heaven and reside in the Southeast, U.S.

9 781966 758051